101
POWERFUL
PROMISES

101
POWERFUL
PROMISES
from
Latter-day
Prophets

WAYNE E. BRICKEY

ℳ®

DESERET BOOK COMPANY
SALT LAKE CITY, UTAH

Library of Congress Cataloging-in-Publication Data

Brickey, Wayne E.
    101 powerful promises from latter-day prophets / Wayne E. Brickey.
        p.   cm.
    Includes bibliographical references and index.
    ISBN 1-59038-335-4 (hardbound : alk. paper)
    1. Christian life—Mormon authors. 2. Church of Jesus Christ of
Latter-day Saints—Doctrines. I. Title: One hundred and one powerful
promises from latter-day prophets. II. Title: One hundred one powerful
promises from latter-day prophets. III. Title.
    BX8656.B745 2004
    248.4'89332—dc22
                                                                    2004016331

Printed in the United States of America   18961
R. R. Donnelley and Sons, Crawfordsville, IN

10   9   8   7   6   5   4   3   2

*To my children, who are
proving in yet another generation
that the promises of God are sure*

CONTENTS

CONTENTS

PART B: PROMISES FOR THE FAMILY

Part C: Promises for the Latter-day Church

Contents

This book is tangible evidence that my wife, Joanne, is a super soul. It also proves that we have uncommonly patient children and uncommonly generous friends.

I am grateful to the people at Deseret Book, who are gracious and professional in every way. I would especially like to mention Cory Maxwell, Chris Schoebinger, Tonya Facemyer, Richard Erickson, and Michael Morris.

We are all indebted to the latter-day prophets. They have paid the price to know the mind and will of God. They have been endlessly honest, gentle, and eloquent to repeat his promises over and over. I have no words to adequately thank them.

INTRODUCTION

*I am very grateful that I can
believe in spiritual realities. . . .
I can believe that there are
powers beyond the material
manifestations of man's intellect
and his force. I am grateful that
God has made it possible for me
to recognize the presence of his
Holy Spirit.*

—Stephen L Richards[1]

There is such a thing as being unsure of the whispering voice of God. This is true of the novice, the trainee, the new traveler, and the self-blinded who hope to ignore promptings that come contrary to their wishes. But the prophets, seers, and revelators are not amateurs; they are expert in detecting the quiet communications of the Spirit. To these of long experience, the voice is unmistakable. Nor do they waver about admitting the truth when it is made known to them. They clearly detect the whispering voice of God, and they are unflinchingly honest.

God has great plans for us, blessings that outstrip our dreams. These are his greatest secrets, but none of them will become realities unless the prophets come to us first and make them known. "Surely the Lord God will do nothing, but he revealeth his secret unto his servants the prophets" (Amos 3:7). God's servants reveal his promises.

The gospel covenant is a panorama of promises full of vast detail. It is the role and the right of prophets to point out the features we

2

need to know. As the angel guided Nephi through his vision, so our prophets say to us, "Behold this part you might not have noticed! And please give your attention to that part of God's mercies to you." Thanks to men in white, we know the best path through latter-day sorrow and peril—a path strangely hidden from the natural man. Thanks be to God that his prophets point out the promises.

The very reason we are in this world is that we believed our Father's promises in the world before. According to the skeptics there, his promises were too grand to be reliable, too expensive to be possible, too generous to believe. For them, there was something suspicious about it all. But you and I chose to believe, and it is now our work to believe again.

How many of God's promises were made to us in the pre-mortal life by messengers instead of by him in person, we cannot say. But in the mortal world, it is clearly his program to send us assurances through fellow mortals, his spokesmen who are right here on the scene with us. This becomes the greatest scripture we have. "The purest word of God, and that least apt to be polluted," Harold B. Lee declared, "is that which comes from the lips of the living prophets."[2]

Dozens of prophets have lived among us in this age of restored truth. None of them has been an amateur, testing and experimenting and wondering about the voice of God. They knew the voice perfectly and spoke without mistake. This book draws on but a few of their thousands of sermons and writings, mining promises sent from heaven through them to us. Perhaps those few—the 101 little chapters or vignettes that follow—may represent the whole in the same way a few sunbeams are samples from the whole spectrum of light.

This book contains four parts. Part A presents promises made to individuals, whereas Part B pertains to families. Part C is about promises for the Church and its latter-day work. Part D focuses on the next life. All of these assurances are part of the great gospel panorama, colored with the kindness and character of a God who never forgets and never fails.

NOTES

1. Stephen L Richards, in Conference Report of The Church of Jesus Christ of Latter-day Saints (Salt Lake City: The Church of Jesus Christ of Latter-day Saints, 1898 to present), October 1931, 45, 46.
2. Harold B. Lee, in *Teachings of Presidents of the Church: Harold B. Lee* (Salt Lake City: The Church of Jesus Christ of Latter-day Saints, 2000), 61.

Part A
Promises for the Individual

You can make a little heaven right here among yourselves, if you want to; and you need not go anywhere else for it. Live your religion, and you will be blessed in time and all eternity. —John Taylor[1]

Heaven can be tasted right here, well before the hereafter. Our religion is much more than an organization or a set of ideas. It is the means of having both heavens—the little one now and the fulness later. The twenty-five promises in Part A assure each individual a taste of heaven while living on earth.

1.

PRAYERS ARE
ANSWERED

Don't worry about your clumsily
expressed feelings. Just talk to
your Father. He hears every
prayer and answers it in His
way.
—Richard G. Scott[2]

Recently a grandmother told the story of twelve-year-old Tamara, who loved to play an old worn-out flute that had been handed down to her. At last the instrument became unusable. Though her family could not afford a new flute, Tamara knew she belonged to a powerful Eternal Father, so she asked for his help.

Christmastime came, and her grandparents happened to attend a party where a drawing was held for donated presents. Another couple, who owned a music store, had just been leaving for the party when they followed an impulse to put a new flute in the car and add it to the gifts. Tamara's grandparents happened to draw the number that won that new flute. What were the odds that such a thing could happen? The odds were certain, if God chose to bring it to pass.

The most basic truth about the universe is that a magnificent, kindly Being upholds all things. And the most basic truth about us is that each of us is his own child, treasured in his sight. "Oh, if you only knew who you are," Boyd K. Packer implored. Then he testified, "You are somebody. Each of you is a son or daughter of God. He will answer your prayers."[3] Once we believe as Tamara does, prayer makes perfect sense.

During our premortal sojourn with God, we spoke to him freely, and he never failed to answer. Now in the mortal test, we do not see him for a little season, and we feel that we do not know him as well. But his interest in us has not diminished one whit. His eyes are still upon us. It is still our privilege to speak with him, and he still promises to answer.

Of course, there can be no communing with him, or with anyone for that matter, unless we are genuine. Prayer is genuine or it isn't prayer. A good parent welcomes every conversation from a sincere child. Otherwise the conversation isn't real. A good teacher welcomes any question as long as the student really wants to hear the answer. Otherwise it isn't really a question.

We are genuine with God when we trust not only that he is "up there somewhere" but also that he is our friend and that he is always right. This is our courtesy, our faith in the Father—giving him credit for what he really is.

And it is only honest to pray with "real intent"—the intention to do his will as soon as he replies (Moroni 10:4). We lean forward, ready to obey. In fact, we already know many of the things he would have us do. If our intent is real, we are already doing those things, even before the next answer comes.

Those who pray genuinely discover again and again that he answers prayers. The same Father who so easily blessed Tamara is the One who hears our every word.

2.
EACH
PERSON MAY
KNOW

*The promise is sure. It is
unlikely that you will hear voices
from heaven, but there will come
a heaven-sent assurance, peaceful and certain. . . . If you will
read the word of the Lord, if you
will serve in his cause, if in
prayer you will talk with him,
your doubts will leave; and shining through all of the confusion
. . . will come the witness of the
Holy Spirit. . . . It is your
opportunity so to know. It is
your obligation so to find out.*
—Gordon B. Hinckley[4]

People in man-made churches must live with uncertainty, or their conviction must rest on tradition, mere habit, or human per-suasion. But as members of Christ's church, we have the right to know from God himself. We had our own testimonies about his church and his diamond truth before we came to this world. Each of us is allowed to have it again.

The laws of God guarantee that a devoted inquiry will not fizzle. As John A. Widtsoe once put it, "Ignorance and doubt always flee before the valiant searcher."[5]

We don't have to walk on a crum-bly surface, unsure about the next step. We don't have to build a life on the ooze of speculation, guess at basic truths, or wonder if the map is right. God isn't hesitant or halfway when he testifies (Helaman 14:4–6). He speaks right to the center of our spirit-selves.

Praying, studying, and obeying constitute a simple offering. Even one who has never tried prayer before can begin, kneeling and asking for the first time, whether, for example, the

Book of Mormon is true. Bruce R. McConkie promised, "It is absolutely guaranteed that sometime between the first and thousandth time this question is asked, every sincere and genuine truth seeker will come to know."[6] Any person who can read may grasp the simple vocabulary of scripture, and one who cannot read may still listen to the message and then study it out in his mind. He who once obeyed little can begin to obey more.

The combination of prayer, study, and obedience calls down a gentle but distinct light. Joseph F. Smith described that light as tangible: "Do this humbly and honestly, and as sure as the Lord lives, I promise you that you will receive the testimony of this work for yourselves. . . . It is something tangible; it is in the power of every man to prove for himself whether we speak the truth."[7]

This light can suddenly evict every shred of doubt at the same time that it pours in its truth. This light is constructive and encouraging, soundly scoring its victory over confusion without the noise of battle.

"I assure you that God will not fail to give you an answer," Delbert L. Stapley assured us. "The warmth of the Spirit will enter your soul and peace and contentment [will enter] into your heart."[8] Testimony comes by the certain, strong voice of peace that men and devils cannot imitate.

Once we are convinced of the truth, we need only be loyal to the light as it grows brighter and brighter—clearing up wider fields of inquiry and chasing dark shadows from our path.

3.
GROWING IN THE PRIVILEGE OF REVELATION

By learning the Spirit of God and understanding it, you may grow into the principle of revelation.
—Joseph Smith[9]

Someday we will meet with Jesus—the ultimate gentleman—in person. For now, gentle undertones of the Holy Ghost guide us to that day. "I have had visions, I have had revelations, I have seen angels," Wilford Woodruff said, "but the greatest of all is that still small voice."[10] Everyone who walks the gospel path has this same experience. The third member of the Godhead walks with them.

What is even more wondrous is this: As we honor our spiritual guide, we become ever more comfortable and skilled at following him. The light of revelation dawns on us more naturally; it is more peaceful, frequent, and distinct. We can *grow* in the principle of revelation.

"When I was first called as stake president," reported one leader, "I wanted to fast about every decision! It seemed that every day I was laboring to know the Lord's will about one thing or another. But over the years the process has become more serene, you might say. His will is clearer to me than ever. Sometimes the promptings settle on my mind before I have a chance to ask. And I'll tell you something else, this is the privilege of every member, not just of the stake president!"

What fosters this growth in the privilege of revelation, this expanding capacity for light? Humility and hunger (3 Nephi 12:6; Enos 1:4). A great prophet assures us, "If we are in an attitude of anxiously seeking the direction of the Spirit, we will receive it." He adds, "There isn't the slightest doubt in my mind concerning this."[11]

Joseph Smith once said the key is simply to "not turn away the small still voice," always keeping our hearts "ready to receive it."[12] The ready heart ignores fearful and selfish impulses, and it takes seriously the positive, uplifting ones. "That which is of Christ does edify," President Hinckley reminds us, "and if we have that feeling of edification, then we may know that the Holy Spirit, the Holy Ghost, is speaking to us."[13]

By contrast, God doesn't pour his light into hearts closed by lack of interest. Seeking hearts grow warmer and larger, but complacent hearts shrink and chill. Indifference prevents growth.

We are drawn to the Holy Ghost as we believe what God has already made known, do what he asks, and love what he loves. By small and patient increases, the companionship becomes "brighter and brighter" (D&C 50:24). Day after day, we grow closer to our bosom friend.

4.

THE MERCIES OF HIS GRACE

The Lord expects us to do all we can to save ourselves, and . . . after we have done all we can to save ourselves, then we can lean upon the mercies of the grace of our Heavenly Father.
—Harold B. Lee[14]

Some people take the plan of salvation too lightly and do not try. Others try too hard. In fact, most faithful people at some time mistakenly think that they have to do more than possible. Thus smitten, they stretch themselves out of shape. They may even invent hardships for others, straining their most crucial relationships. This view is wrong because it is not guided by faith in the wisdom of God; it does not quite trust his simple requests.

Sometimes it is oddly convenient—selfish in a way—to live a life of extremes and distortions rather than to keep things balanced. But the Lord is pleased with a life lived in balance. He asks that we do what we can and no more. He will do the "more" part.

There are many versions of doing all we can, and each of them is balanced. The imbalance comes when we mistake our priorities. The mother who runs down to the family history library and labors there while the children arrive from school to a motherless home may think she is doing all she can do. But perhaps she is not being honest with what she knows in her heart.

Down the street might be a person with no little ones at home. She may be ignoring some quiet urgings to go to that same library and help her ancestors. Hers may be yet another life out of balance, not doing all she can do.

He who made us does not ask us to go beyond the limits he has set for our bodies and our minds, our budgets and our families. Denying these boundaries or forever fussing over them is a silly distraction. Even when the job changes, the work remains the same: to give all of one's self in one's sphere. Our offering is then a full one. It triggers the grace of God—the peace and approval and ready smiles of heaven.

But if we then stop along the path to cajole or scourge ourselves for not giving more, we have at that moment stopped giving altogether, turning inwardly. We do not and cannot then detect those smiles. Perhaps in our distrust and blind overreaching, we don't quite deserve them.

New battles are prone to erupt in the mortal adventure, and we must be willing to shift to new fields. The next field may be smaller than we expected. By faith we adjust. We keep doing what we can, rather than daydreaming about other missions. In the process, we sense our Father's heart filling with approval.

In a time sure to come, our opportunities and powers will expand dramatically. Our "all" will then be great, and we will go on doing all we can, just as we now do in the narrow spot of mortal time. "When a man keeps all the law that is revealed, according to his strength, his substance, and his ability," Joseph F. Smith declared, "though what he does may be little, it is just as acceptable in the sight of God as if he were able to do a thousand times more."[15]

5.
THE GIFT OF NEWNESS

If one's testimony is strong enough, he repents and obeys the commandments. By such obedience he receives divine forgiveness which remits sin. Thus he is converted to a newness of life. His spirit is healed.

—Marion G. Romney[16]

If we act upon the light we have, we are made new—spotless before our Father and filled with his life. The promise even applies to people with the toughest habits and deepest wounds. "That which they had been led to believe could not be changed, will be changed, and they will feel the power of the redemption of Christ," declared Boyd K. Packer. "Their burden will be lifted and the pain healed up. That is what the Atonement of Christ is all about."[17]

Our condition on entering this world—new and pure—symbolizes the fresh beginning. Rebirth is recommended not only for the beginner but also for the gospel veteran. No matter how far we have come down the path, newness is always possible. The Healer is willing to cure yet another spot.

Whenever injured—whether by personal sin or abuse from another—the human spirit is too big and complex to be easily restored. It is a job for the great Christ, who picks up the pieces and reassembles the whole, as in remaking a shattered vase. He does not merely glue it up, of course. He fuses the pieces as one, shard by shard. Whether in nature or in the natural man, he works by many small miracles.

The sequence is guided by his intricate wisdom. The pace is set by our daily permission. And every moment spent in the slow and sacred healing process is time in the arms of Christ.

He will not abandon his holy task until it is complete, until the vessel is perfect and whole. When he has at last wiped away all tears, they will not start to flow again (Revelation 21:4). His miracle does not fade any more than a great tree can revert to a tiny seed.

Just as the process has a distinct fulness, it has a distinct beginning. One might even notice that moment, as Enos did, when the relief and assurance start to spread and conquer and make new (Enos 1:6–7). The beginning can be in whatever *now* we decide it will be. When we turn to Christ, when we face up to his truth—his true gospel and true church and true prophets and true commandments—the true healing begins.

At times, we sense the Healer beckon. "If you have felt impressions to be free of burdens caused by yourself or others, those promptings are an invitation from the Redeemer," Richard G. Scott testified. "Act upon them now."[18] The newborn baby comes into this world clumsy and weak and unknowing, but the crucial thing is that it comes. Birth is not about feeling poised or polished. If we do not feel ready, we can, in our clumsy way, repent now anyway and make the gift of newness ours.

6.
STABILITY AND PURPOSE

They who reach down into the depths of life where, in the stillness, the voice of God is heard, have the stabilizing power which carries them poised and serene through the hurricane of difficulties.

—Spencer W. Kimball[19]

Our day—with its confusion and noise, its blurry, dark, and whirling pace—is much like a hurricane. The steadying voice is not found shouting above it all. Stability speaks in the quiet interior, "in the stillness" where prayer begins and the testimony of Christ is kept, that familiar chamber where we detect truth and where we chose to do the right thing.

In that place of patient hearing, we find out what the Master would like us to do. There, we can avoid getting tangled in other things. There, we decide to do his short list of tasks. There, we resist adding to our marching orders, avoiding the tendency to dwarf his list with a longer list of our own.

If we fail to listen in those depths, if we ignore the interior voice, if we indulge ourselves in self-appointed missions, we will soon complain that we have too many things to do. And then a hundred hours in a day will not be enough. The truth is, we don't need more time for doing things. We need more vision about what few things to do.

Evan was a young man always in a rush. His friends admired him because he was so involved in everything, but his parents had another view. They rarely saw him, and when they did he didn't seem happy. Finally his mother suggested that he "get off the fast track" for a while every day. He accepted the challenge. He spent some of that time in prayer and some of it in the scriptures.

"It's the best thing I've ever done. I still do it," Evan said a few years later. "I'm one of those 'racehorse' types. I'll probably be that way all my life. My secret to happiness is to get off the race-track every day. When I pray, I really pray. When I study the scriptures, I pay attention. At some point in this routine, I realized I was listening to the Spirit. It fills a spot in me that nothing else can reach. And, when I get back on the track, I have better judgment about how to spend my time."

Nora spent the last years of her life in a care center. Her mind, easily crowded and disoriented during that time, was beset by worries. She had children with troubled marriages. She had a grandson who frequently found himself on the wrong side of the law. She had a close relative who faced financial woes associated with a shrinking bank account.

In addition, Nora's health presented her with daily discomfort. Her visiting teacher, unable to change these things, finally struck on a way to help. She spent an hour each day with Nora, reading from the scriptures and Church magazines. This practice didn't remove Nora's burdens, but somehow they no longer distressed her. Nora was equal to them. She handled the troubled twilight of her life with poise and peace.

The voice of God, whispering beneath the hurricane, doesn't just tell us what to do and what to skip. It teaches us who we are and who we don't have to be. By assuring us of our high origin and purpose, it makes us stronger than the storms.

7.

THE DELICIOUS FRUIT

You and those you love will receive the word of God by obeying it. That will allow them to feel His love. That is one of the great blessings of the gift of the Holy Ghost. When we feel that love we can know that our course in life is approved of God. That is the feast of the delicious fruit described in the Book of Mormon.
—Henry B. Eyring[20]

The wrong kind of *fun* is expensive and usually evaporates before the payments come due. *Joy,* on the other hand, is purchased ahead of time and at bargain prices. It is whole, connected with all of the important things, rather than fragmented and irrelevant. Joy lasts and lasts. It pays dividends.

We have the whole cloth of happiness when we know we are on the right path and when we trust that knowledge. We have joy when we realize that our life is acceptable to God. We have joy when we know that we are ready to return to him when called, and that in the meantime we are ready for action in his service. Such joy is the feast of faithfulness, the sensation our Father wishes us to have all the time.

Lasting joy has never come by lavish treats or spectacular feats, or even by heavenly signs and wonders. Speaking by authority and wisdom, John A. Widtsoe cautioned, "No one is nearer the Lord because of some unusual spiritual experience."[21] The particular nearness we crave is like the nearness we felt in the premortal life.

In that home, it had nothing to do with the dramatic or sensational. It came because of our loyalty (Abraham 3:22–23).

J. Reuben Clark pleaded, "Let all your activities, everything that you do in life, let them all lead unto this great fundamental fact, that Jesus is the Christ, the Messiah." We can never be far from him if we make him central and thereby merit the promise that "there shall come to you more satisfaction in living and following this life than anything else you could do in this world."[22] It was so with Enos, who "rejoiced in it above that of the world" (Enos 1:26).

We can live in our surroundings without being subject to them (John 14:27). For this reason, we could "thrust a man into prison and bind him with chains," but if he is "filled with the comfort and with the glory of eternity," said Brigham Young, ". . . that prison is a palace to him."[23] This is a principle with a promise. It amounts to saying that genuine kings and queens— true sons and daughters of the Heavenly King—transcend circumstance. They are in royal courts wherever they go. We may know them by the fruits of their royal works, including their delicious fruit of joy.

8.
AN HONORED TIME

Strive in your homes, and teach others, to take some time of each day to have a quiet hour. . . . Tune in with God and discuss with Him problems that are too much for human understanding, too great for human strength.

—Harold B. Lee[24]

A daily period of devotion and inspiration holds blessings we cannot gain in any other way. God has so designed mortality that spiritual needs resemble physical ones: the tissues need nutrition and rebuilding every day.

But that vital hour—a time to resecure our live connection with heaven and to get direction for the hours ahead—seems harder to set aside than time to eat and sleep. It must be scheduled and protected by habit and routine. To honor that space of time is to honor him whom we seek. He responds by honoring us. He often fills that space, and the whole day, with his influence.

While the time of day will be different in some situations, early morning is best for most of us. "I get up early in the morning," Harold B. Lee said. How early? "Five o'clock, when my mind and spirit are clear and rested." What did he do at that hour? "I meditate. You can come closer to the Lord than you imagine when you learn to meditate. . . . Don't get so busy that you don't have time to meditate. Take the time."[25] When he says to take the time, he certainly means that we should protect that time by making an appointment and being loyal to it.

"But rising early means going to bed early," someone might say. "That's fine for President Lee and others, but I happen to be one of those people who can't sleep if they go to bed early." Perhaps you know such a person; perhaps you are such a person. The answer is simple: If we will get up early every day for several days, we will soon find ourselves sleepy at an earlier hour of the evening. It works like magic! Fine habits often call for a time of patience and faith (D&C 88:124).

One of the hardest things we can ever do is go to bed early each night, night after night, for weeks and months and years. Yet, this one practice can secure some of our greatest blessings. It swings open a door to the quiet and powerful hours of the next day, the early morning when all is clean and clear. At night we pay for the blessing, and in the morning we receive it.

Whatever the hour may be, President Hinckley called it "a wondrous experience with thoughts and words of things divine."[26] Feeding the spirit and communing with heaven is a covenant thing to do, an obvious part of our discipleship. That honored time soon becomes a daily fortress filled with treasure.

9.
TRAINED BY SCRIPTURE

People who study the scriptures
get a dimension to their life that
nobody else gets and that can't
be gained in any way except by
studying the scriptures. There's
an increase in faith and a desire
to do what's right and a feeling
of inspiration and understand-
ing that comes to people who
study the gospel—meaning par-
ticularly the Standard Works—
and who ponder the principles,
that can't come in any other
way.
—Bruce R. McConkie[27]

The greatest blessings require that we immerse ourselves in our Father's words. To have the scriptures nearby and yet turn to other resources for solace and power is an enormous loss. For those who know better, it is a foolish error.

"How could a person possibly become what he is not thinking?" asked Spencer W. Kimball.[28] It's amazing what happens within us when we turn on the inside lights. To regularly immerse our minds in the thoughts of God himself is to make a wise investment in our personal growth.

The standard works are so fundamental that, in the words of Rudger Clawson, they could "form a solid basis from which and by which to regenerate the world."[29] If from the standard works we could build the world's base of knowledge afresh, we could certainly build anything else as well from the same foundation.

Of course, the daily immersion isn't about mind and thought only. Besides the written and printed version of the word, we have the whispered and prompted version. One may be quoted; the other is fundamentally quiet. But they have much in common, and one leads to the other. Scripture study prepares us for personal inspiration by training the heart.

Detecting power in the scriptures requires that we see beyond the written word's literary beauty, good advice, and support for our views. Searched properly, they become a light that humbles and cleanses and lifts our very center, training our hearts to detect the whispered word even when no book is present.

We need to study with a kind of care, a certain hunger and longing. If we attend too heavily to the facts and details found in the written word, we may miss the taste of living water that the word bore when it was first brought forth. The word was born as a prompting before it ever went to print, and that prompting power still attends the image on page or screen or on sound wave in the air. There, in black and white, awaits a feast of truth and light.

No wonder Joseph Smith advised us, "Search the scriptures. . . . When men receive their instruction from Him that made them, they know how He will save them."[30] When our minds and hearts have this complete knowledge and when we are thoroughly trained in it, then, J. Golden Kimball promised, "You shall hear a voice behind you saying, 'This is the way, walk ye in it.'"[31]

10.

A Diamond Among the Standard Works

I bless you with increased understanding of the Book of Mormon. I promise you that from this moment forward, if we will daily sup from its pages and abide by its precepts, God will pour out upon each child of Zion and the Church a blessing hitherto unknown. . . . Of this I bear solemn witness.

—Ezra Taft Benson[32]

It is one thing to draw living water from the scriptures generally; it is another thing to select from the scriptures one volume from which those waters flow most steadily and forcefully. But in this matter there is no doubt. The Book of Mormon is in a category by itself, even among the standard works.

Joseph Smith called the Book of Mormon "the keystone of our religion."[33] This suggests that we can establish the truth of the restored gospel by first verifying that the Book of Mormon is true. Its validity solidly supports and confirms a thousand other truths.

But that famous statement from the Prophet Joseph offers us another insight about this keystone: We can "get nearer to God by abiding by its precepts, than by any other book."[34] The Book of Mormon has been brought forth at great expense to heaven and earth for more reasons than just corroborating the truth of the latter-day work. It is also the keystone of our spiritual life, the central tool for drawing close to God. Diamond-like—or perhaps Urim and

Thummim-like—it captures and dispenses the light of heaven as no other book. In a dark and dreary day, this book is to be a source of power to the disciples of Christ, helping them to become Saints, mortals filled with light (1 Nephi 6:4; 2 Nephi 33:4, 10–11).

It is no surprise, then, that Ezra Taft Benson would promise supernal blessings to those who "daily sup from its pages and abide by its precepts." It may also explain why, on another occasion, he called it a "great sifter." As he observed on that occasion, there is an evident "difference in discernment, in insight, conviction, and spirit between those who know and love the Book of Mormon and those who do not."[35]

Nor is it surprising that President Hinckley testified, "If you will prayerfully read the Book of Mormon, regardless of how many times you have previously read it, there will come into your heart an added measure of the Spirit of the Lord."[36] People living amid growing difficulty need an added measure of power.

For ages past, God was laying plans, guiding events, and grooming prophets so that this latter-day supplement could be published. It now rests safely in our hands. To continually "get nearer to God," we need but open it and then open our hearts every day of our mortal lives to each successive message on its pages. This shining stone is in our hands for just that reason.

11.

BE ASSERTIVE WITH TEMPTATIONS

When you feel as though you would burst, tell the old boiler to burst, and just laugh at the temptation. . . . If you will continue to do that, you will soon be . . . masters of yourselves.
—Brigham Young[37]

When Joseph Smith went to his death at Carthage, he spoke of being innocent of offense toward God and man (D&C 135:4). He didn't get a clear conscience by doing nothing or by doing his own thing. If we are to return to our Father with such a conscience, we too will need to be assertive in the mortal fight with sin. We are entitled to say no, firmly and everlastingly, to Satan's every intrusion.

Richard G. Scott shared an important secret to purity when he said, "Strength comes from making no exceptions to your principles."[38] Of course, we first have to be clear about our principles, making sure we get them from the perfect source. And then comes the sturdy, attentive, life-long work of making no exceptions to them.

In the face of each temptation, we pray for strength and put up our full resistance. We never give a dishonest little nod to compromise. We never say to ourselves that we can always repent tomorrow or that this particular sin isn't so bad. We never listen to the darker voice always asking if we are willing to give up yet another pint of lifeblood from our souls. We do as Jesus did: We simply give no heed to the temptation (D&C 20:22).

If a temptation is so sore that we begin to view the chance to sin as a golden opportunity of some kind, we can be sure it is all a lie. We must let it slide by without a glance. The devil likes us to make a big fuss over him, to bite our nails, and to debate the matter endlessly, staring at temptation from every angle. It is far better to immediately turn our backs and get out, to turn our minds from it and go on.

"God has given to me, and to no one else, the keeping of this house and this doorway," we say to the insidious, intruding salesman. "I will not have you come in and make your presentation. I will not listen to any of it on the porch. I will not hear of your bargain prices. Not one of your products interests me. I will not listen to the first word. Do not speak. I am neither your customer nor your prospect. I give you no permission to be near this house. Depart."

And then we shut the door and turn our attention to worthy things. After each triumph, righteousness comes more easily the next time.

Such episodes have an effect on all eternity. Therefore, we react to each dark inducement as if it were our last stand, our last battle. Someday, one of those confrontations with temptation will actually prove to be our last. We will enter the higher world as quiet victors over the adversary. Though it sometimes may have bruised our heels to do so, we will have given him no heed. We will have trodden his head underfoot (Genesis 3:15; Moses 4:21).

12.
SLOW DOWN, LOOK WITHIN, AND OBEY

When you are tempted, buffeted, and step out of the way inadvertently; when you are overtaken in a fault, or commit an overt act unthinkingly; when you are full of evil passion, and wish to yield to it, then stop and let the spirit, which God has put into your tabernacles, take the lead. If you do that, I will promise that you will overcome all evil, and obtain eternal lives.
—Brigham Young[39]

Despite the popular notion that people just can't be expected to govern themselves, David O. McKay testified that each of us "can control his mind, can choose what seems the best, no matter how attractive the opposite force may be." Then he added, "There is a crying need today to have this truth heralded throughout the land."[40]

Temptation comes to us physically. The channels of the spirit, on the other hand, are far stronger. The noble and eternal part of us ought to be in charge and ought to take the lead. If this realignment—this decision to ignore the natural man and yield to the enticings of the Holy Spirit—requires a bit of time, so be it (Mosiah 3:19). What better way to use up our minutes and hours in the only mortal probation we will ever have? We forego no blessing by pausing to let our interior monitor ascend to the helm. We only forego the regrets and setbacks that attend transgression.

We gain wisdom during those important pauses. In the classroom of our own inner world, we are learning about the nature of God. He never acts from mere self-interest. He is thoughtful and knowing, always acting on godly principles. We imitate him somewhat when we obey the quiet voice of goodness he has transplanted from his being to ours (D&C 84:47–48).

It was as if Brigham Young was sharing a trade secret when he suggested, "Never [permit] yourself to commit an act unless the Spirit of God within you justifies you in doing it."[41] On another occasion he said, "Decide in your own minds that your will and judgment shall be none other than the will and judgment of the Spirit of God, and you will then go and sin no more."[42] This is the secret of the righteous (D&C 132:37). It is how they manage to keep doing what is right.

Joseph Smith once said, "In obedience there is joy and peace unspotted."[43] Undiluted happiness awaits those who let their higher faculties prevail in critical moments. Sometimes this means to prayerfully slow things down, as when the prudent driver watches for signs at a crucial, unfamiliar intersection. We will always obey the Lord if we permit our spirit to join forces with his spirit.

13.
QUIETLY BECOMING A MASTERPIECE

Men and women who . . . humbly plod along, doing their duty, . . . who help look after the poor; and who honor the holy Priesthood, who do not run into excesses, who are prayerful in their families, and who acknowledge the Lord in their hearts, they will build up a foundation that the gates of hell cannot prevail against.

—Joseph F. Smith[44]

It is wonderful to know that we can live the highest ideals and gain the greatest success without calling any attention to ourselves. God can make a masterpiece out of any member of his family, and this he can do without the sound of hammer and chisel.

One of the quiet characteristics of a masterpiece human being is *happiness*, which, as Joseph Smith said, "is the object and design of our existence."[45] Every feature of our design was created with happiness in mind, and happiness was made possible with us in mind. Perhaps there are moments when you or I suppose we are one of the unhappy exceptions—a defective model maybe. But we should remember that mortal life isn't a good sample of eternity. We are in a special period right now—a peculiar test we will never repeat again—to discover just what we will care about when we are feeling a bit defective. If we will be faithful, the test itself will help us become a masterpiece.

Masterpiece human beings have a good track record with their own conscience. They neither hush nor ignore its urgings, and this is reason for their happiness. "The reward of a man's conscience," said Heber J. Grant, "is far better than the praise of those who cannot read his heart."[46]

We grow more perfect "in proportion to the heed and diligence given to the light communicated from heaven to the intellect." In these words, Joseph Smith was saying that heaven does send light to each person, into that part of us—the "intellect"—that thinks and reacts, forms attitudes, and makes decisions. To the degree that a person is loyal to the impulses of that private light, "the clearer are his views, and the greater his enjoyments, till he has overcome the evils of his life and lost every desire for sin; and like the ancients, arrives at that point of faith where he is wrapped in the power and glory of his Maker and is caught up to dwell with Him."[47]

The promise of might and nobility is not restricted to people of a certain lineage or language or income or wardrobe. The light of Christ is shared with all, regardless of whether the world has ever heralded them or even heard of them. We can be sure that the great Father of our race looks on with tender interest. Whether by great, quick strides or painstaking baby steps, each soul is free to tread the way to perfection (Moroni 7:16; D&C 93:31). On that lighted path, all great beings have traveled.

14.
A FOUNDATION FOR AGES TO COME

By virtue of the authority in us vested as the First Presidency of the Church, we . . . call upon you to keep, day in and day out, the way of strictest chastity, through which only can God's choice gifts come to you and His Spirit abide with you. How glorious is he who lives the chaste life. He walks unfearful in the full glare of the noon day sun. . . . He is loved by the Lord, for he stands without blemish. The exaltations of eternities await his coming.

—The First Presidency[48]

Chastity is a fountain of personal force in every life, but we may not be able to fully explain this until we can closely observe that sector of the universe that is currently closed to our view—the realm of spirit. Still, as Joseph F. Smith pointed out, "There appears to be a something beyond and above the reasons apparent to the human mind why chastity brings strength and power to the peoples of the earth, but it is so."[49]

So basic is the strength of a chaste life that it affects everything and lasts forever. "Youth is the time to lay the foundation for our homes," David O. McKay said. "I assure you that self-mastery, not indulgence, is the virtue that contributes to the virility of manhood and to the beauty of womanhood."[50] That principle may be surprising to some, but special people prove it daily in real life.

One who comes to mind was a boy, not outstanding in the eyes of his peers, who was virtuous in every way. Steadily the years have showered upon him the graces of human greatness. He didn't seek those strengths for which so many now depend on him. The fruits of purity have simply appeared, right where they belong. Few noticed as an unremarkable boy transformed into a remarkable man, but had we understood the principle, we would have expected it all along.

Enriching our gender characteristics—such as the power of woman to nurture and the power of man to provide and pre-side—is a project based on eternal law. Every step toward the glory of eternal womanhood or the might of eternal manhood is made in pure love. On the other hand, selfishness—the essence of lust—spoils everything. The power of gender and the force of the human soul are diminished, not increased, by promiscuity. Ironic, isn't it? The foundation for an invincible and happy life is laid long before that life fully unfolds.

Among the host of things we cling to in this life, few are vital. We can even afford to give up physical life itself, as we will all someday realize. (For every mortal, that expense is already in the budget!) What, then, is vital? The foundation, of course—the hope and health of our souls (3 Nephi 12:28–30; Matthew 10:28, 39). In the day-by-day moments, choosing to think and live with purity, we make a foundation that will last the ages.

15.
THE SHIELD OF VIRTUE

The keeping of the seventh commandment is such a vital shield! By lowering or losing that shield, the much-needed blessings of heaven are lost. No person or nation can prosper for long without those blessings. Strange, in a time otherwise obsessed with entitlements, how little concern there is over our becoming entitled to the blessings of heaven.

—Neal A. Maxwell[51]

There is a special protection for parrying off the fiery, poison-tipped darts of a raging Satan. It is what the scriptures call the shield of faith (Ephesians 6:16; D&C 27:17). In a day when fiery darts fill the air, we cannot afford to let the shield lay useless at our feet. Yet that is the result of unchastity.

Faith believes what is made known to the spirit within. It accepts this special kind of knowledge, which is so real and yet, in the mortal body, so easy to disregard. The person who is preoccupied with physical appearance and sensation is prone to miss or deny spiritual reality. As Jesus pointed out more than once, a carnal approach to belief (insisting on a physical sign) indicates a carnal attitude about everything else, including the sanctity of sex (Matthew 12:39; 16:4). The carnal mind is largely disabled, blind to the sacredness of sacred things.

So, unless sight is restored, the carnal mind is bound to deny the faith. Satan's slanders, ploys, and poisons seem acceptable enough. The carnal mind doesn't get it. It has no shield.

To use a mild Hollywood example, Indiana Jones is immune to certain horrific, vengeful spirits locked in the ark of the covenant (itself, a strange distortion of sacred things). He is protected because he knows when to look and when not to look! But this "hero" is also portrayed as a man of blatant, unhesitant unchastity. Of course, a basic truth has been badly twisted here, for heroism lies not in wild adventures but in purity of life.

Had ruthless spirits of the dead really come raging out of that old box, Indiana would not have stood a chance against them. His private life was the problem. He had no shield. Such are not the sort of Joneses we should keep up with.

In the Sermon on the Mount, Jesus clearly taught that even the simplest act—such as looking at someone—is wrong when driven by lust (Matthew 5:28; 3 Nephi 12:28). A lustful view on the world is narrow-minded, demeaning, and addictive. Lust cancels the promise of protection. In contrast, chastity qualifies us for spiritual power, aligns us with uplifting friends, bestows a clear conscience, and entitles us to the company of angels. Day by day it frees our eyes and thoughts, allowing us to look upon other human beings with respect, rather than as objects of selfish interest or intruding curiosity.

President Hinckley assures us that "our safety lies in the virtue of our lives."[52] Chastity is the most powerful defense to be found on the mortal battlefield. Against a storm of deadly arrows, we are absolutely safe as long as the modest shield stays in place.

16.
THOUGHT AND DESTINY

This relationship of character to thought cannot be too strongly emphasized. How could a person possibly become what he is not thinking? Nor is any thought, when persistently entertained, too small to have its effect. The "divinity that shapes our ends" is indeed in ourselves. It is one's very self.
—Spencer W. Kimball [53]

In this principle we find both a promise and a warning—good news and bad news. The promise is that we will grow to be just as majestic as our thoughts dictate, and nothing less. But the warning is that we will shrink to be just as petty as our thoughts dictate, and nothing more! Our destiny isn't decided merely by what we write on a piece of paper, what we proclaim, or how we dress. It comes from the things that fill our heads.

"Sow a thought and reap a degree of glory," we might say. But we might better say, "Sow a long train of thought, a theme of thought for a lifetime." Even better, if thoughts are like seeds, "Sow and nourish and watch over and then act upon those thoughts. *Then* comes a degree of glory" (D&C 88:28–29). So how do we manage to steadily plant such destiny-creating, glory-begetting seeds? We begin by screening out certain other seeds.

Many a farmer has planted a whole truck full of seed only to learn a few weeks later that the batch was contaminated with a tiny portion of weed seeds. An elderly farmer in Idaho related an extreme case:

"A fellow came through the country a few generations ago, selling a specially bred strain of pasture grass. Johnsongrass he called it. Guaranteed it would grow like a weed. That was true enough. Never occurred to us that it *was* a weed. But it was. Still is."

Reckoned by the life cycle of weed grasses, johnsongrass has now propagated itself for many generations, spreading to countless places where it was never invited. It has no nutritional value for cattle. It is unsightly. Its roots are gnarly and formidable, growing thick and running deep.

Many are the themes of thought, whether false or vulgar or merely distracting, that take over like johnsongrass, spreading into souls, choking off all other roots, blocking the light, stealing the space, preventing good fruit, canceling destiny.

President McKay counseled students, "Keep yourselves free from the tendencies that will arouse your physical passions, and you will have increased intellectual energy."[54] That purity can improve the intellect is a wonderful promise but not a new one. We remember the mental and physical blessings God promised in D&C 88:124, conditioned on our discipleship.

Where shall we buy our seed? The Source of all good has advised us to sow into our minds only the very finest, that which is stored in the "best books" (D&C 88:118). With valuable advice like that, there awaits us an array too wide and too rich to measure, leading eventually to a destiny too wonderful to comprehend. And it leaves us no time to waste on planting weeds.

17.
A DAY TO RESTORE US

The Sabbath day is given throughout the generations of man for a perpetual covenant. It is a sign between the Lord and his children forever. . . . It is a day not for affliction and burden but for rest and righteous enjoyment . . . a day to restore us to our spiritual stature.

—Spencer W. Kimball [55]

Rarely do we notice the little losses we suffer as each day the fallen world leaves its soil and fatigue upon our spirits. Even Isaiah, so remarkable among the prophets, had to admit that living in the midst of an unclean people had taken its toll on him (Isaiah 6:5). Days may pass before we see the damage: less peace, more difficulty making wise decisions, less tolerance for weakness in others, more susceptibility to temptation. As with the body when it weakens, the spirit can lose force and become woozy during exertion, stumbling along without focus. After a week of this, we need renewal.

Consider the gloom that would result if there were no relieving of burdens, no regular break to clean and make repairs, no chance for mercy and reinstatement, no special time for seeing clearly again. More than we can measure, the Sabbath keeps us and our hopes alive. We might say that as the Restoration refreshed a failing world, so the Sabbath, week after week, refreshes each individual who honors it. It is a day for personal restoration. If we lack enthusiasm for this day of renewal, perhaps it is because we don't discern our own need.

The Sabbath law is easier to keep—automatic in fact—if we are sensitive to spiritual realities. "The reason the Sabbath day is so hard to live for so many people," suggested Spencer W. Kimball, "is that it is still written on tablets of stone rather than being written in their hearts."[56] If this privilege is written in our hearts, we will need no stony law to demand that we hold still while someone feeds us. Instead, hunger will draw us to the Lord's table. We will want to sit down with the family and feast, enjoying the companionship of other covenant keepers.

But do the hours of worship make an actual difference? Can a whole day of spiritual attention be worth the time? We might ask if the Restoration was worth all the strain, all the lost property and life. Does a meal and good rest make a difference to the spent and weary body? We might ask if there is a difference between night and day.

When I was young, I longed to work with wild animals. Finally there came the opportunity of a lifetime: I was offered a job with a large, world-renowned zoo. The pay and benefits were excellent, the career opportunities promising. I glanced down a moment to pinch myself on the arm, just to be sure I wasn't dreaming. Then the interviewer said, "Of course, you know you will have to work on Sundays." I looked up, unable to conceal my shock. "It's our biggest day," he explained. "Sundays are a must."

Has it made a difference to the eternal part of me that I turned down that job two thousand Sabbaths ago? In answer, I ask: Has the Restoration—with all its truth, fellowship, standards, hope, promises, and power—lifted mankind? It is as the difference between night and day.

18.
BLESSING OUR THINGS

From the creation story we notice a special connection between the physical world and the Sabbath. On the seventh day, God was "refreshed" after his creative labors (Exodus 31:17). And on that day he blessed all the "things" he had made (Moses 3:2–3).

A physical creation shorn of its higher purposes would be a silly project, not worth the bother. But when the physical is partnered with the spiritual—that is a different matter. When combined with the spiritual in a worthy way, the physical is blessed, whole, and holy (D&C 29:31–34).

As apprentices in the Creator's great plan, we are invited to put our own little temporal worlds in order as he would do if he were in our position (Luke 16:13; Matthew 25:21–23). This is a gesture, a token of our priorities. On the first day of the week, we put first things first. We put the Lord of the Sabbath first.

Joseph Fielding Smith's statement offers only one illustration. If the storeowner should close his doors on the Sabbath, we can imagine other brave possibilities. For example, we would not encourage a store to stay open, especially for unnecessary business, even if the store isn't ours. Above all, we remember that the Sabbath isn't just about closing stores. It is a day to open ourselves and our doors to the *Lord's* business. The promise is that we will be blessed "more abundantly" (Mosiah 18:10). A host of Book of Mormon prophets put it this way: We will "prosper in the land" (1 Nephi 4:13; 2 Nephi 1:20; Mosiah 2:22; Alma 37:13).

Perhaps in my lesser moments I will say, "I don't know about all this. Why not let the Lord take care of *his* things, and let me take care of *mine*." But no. My kingdom of "things"—the makings of a garage sale and nothing more—hardly compares to his kingdom of majesty and totality. And yet he offers to switch roles in a way. If I will take care of his kingdom, he pledges to take care of mine! And all the "things" I need will be thrown into the bargain by his almighty hand (Matthew 6:33; JST, Matthew 6:38).

One couple in the grocery business, haunted by the question for years, finally sat down and decided to let their store sit dark and idle on Sundays. They did not suddenly see greater profits. Instead, former customers went elsewhere to shop, and profits fell off dangerously. They revisited their decision, this time staring at the face of financial disaster. They chose to hold their course. After several losing months, they were forced out of business. But of course, the end of that chapter was but the beginning of another.

"We never had such peace before," the wife said. "It just felt right, even when we were losing money. We have different employment now. The losses are in the past. They don't matter. We have what we need. We're serving in the Church and we're happy."

God cares about tokens. The way we treat his day is a token of how we feel about our things and the Father's things, about our business and the Father's business.

19.
OPEN THE WINDOWS

*If you will be honest with the
Lord, paying your tithing and
keeping His commandments,
He will not only bless you with
the light and inspiration of His
Holy Spirit, but you will be
blessed in dollars and cents; . . .
and the Lord will pour out temporal blessings upon you in
great abundance.*

—Heber J. Grant[58]

Trusting in her strong testimony of the Book of
Mormon, a young woman by
the name of Isabel joined the Church.
But as a single mother barely surviv-
ing on tiny wages, she began to waver
when it came to paying tithing for the
first time. The missionaries had testified of their own experiences with the
law, but she wondered if the windows
of heaven could open for her in the
Chilean highlands.

Isabel hinted at her worries in a
conversation with the Relief Society
president of her branch. The following
Sunday, the president asked the sisters
if any of them would like to stand and
share their convictions about the law
of tithing. What happened then could
have taken place in thousands of other
wards and branches in any given meeting. As she walked home that day, testimony after testimony ringing in her
mind, Isabel knew that the question
was not about the law of tithing but
only about whether she would have the
faith to live it.

By long experience, we know that
"faithful payment of tithing even by
the very poor," Dallin H. Oaks said,

eventually "raises people out of poverty and dependency."[59] Our Father sometimes permits his children to live in deplorable circumstances, but when they respond to his laws, he soon lifts them out and sets them on the road to liberty and poise.

Tithing is a token of honesty, really. At any increase of our funds, there is always that tenth part that is not ours at all. This added portion is the Lord's property, slipped into our hands as a kind of test. To retain it is to "rob God," to seize what never belonged to us to begin with (Malachi 3:8). Considered in this way, tithing is not an expense, for we can hardly *spend* what is not ours. To render it up is the only honest thing to do.

What is the reward for this honesty? Millions of faithful tithe payers can verify that the blessings are twofold: both spirit and substance are affected by this special law. The promise above from Heber J. Grant mentions light on one hand and dollars and cents on the other. Light pours down through the windows of heaven while at the same time temporal blessings surge up from a cooperating earth. Tithing is a surefire investment (D&C 64:23). In the math of faith, to pay a tenth of our increase *is* increase.

This law helps us elude the ultimate poverty: the plague of materialism—the bizarre tendency to set one's heart upon money and the few poor things it can buy. It is one thing to need things but quite another to be in love with them and rest one's happiness upon them!

"The man who depends upon his wealth shall be left finally without it," said a wise apostle. "Whether or not he is so unfortunate as to lose it in this life he shall leave it when he goes hence and may walk the streets of the spirit world the poorest beggar in the realm."[60]

In every sense, cheerfully living the law of tithing is a gain of every kind.

20.
A LAW OF GENEROSITY

Multiple blessings result when we pay a generous fast offering. The payment of a generous fast offering, which will bless the lives of the poor and needy, will also make our prayers more meaningful and bring additional spiritual and temporal blessings into our lives.
—Howard W. Hunter[61]

Church donations are categorized as "tithes" on one hand and as "offerings" on the other. When we tithe, we refund the *Lord's* money. This honesty permits him to bless us. But when we make offerings, we give him *our* money. This is not just honesty but generosity, and it allows him to bless us with his own greater generosity.

By our offerings, we answer the cries of our fellow beings. The kinds of offerings vary, as do the needs. But the basic and essential offering combines our hunger and prayer with our generosity—the fast offering. Our leaders often suggest that we try to pay a generous fast offering.

Just as Jesus watched the offerings in ancient times, he continues to behold "how the people cast money into the treasury" (Mark 12:41). He measures hearts, seeing just how kindly each person responds to the plight of others.

Spencer W. Kimball lamented, "Sometimes we have . . . figured that we had for breakfast one egg and that cost so many cents and then we give that to the Lord." He then suggested,

"We ought to be very, very generous [and] . . . give, instead of the amount saved by our two meals of fasting, perhaps much, much more—ten times more where we are in a position to do it." He reiterated the ancient promise: "We shall increase our own prosperity both spiritually and temporally."[62]

Earl and Lynn were a young married couple attending college when Earl found himself unemployed. Not only were they without income, but they were also without medical insurance to cover the birth of the child they were expecting. The first Sunday of the month was at hand. It was natural to fast and pray. But what of the offering? How liberal should it be? They had heard President Kimball's statement, and they somehow knew the time had come for faith to take the form of generosity. They decided on an amount many times their previous offerings.

Within the week, Earl had a strange thought to stop at a particular business that recently told him it had no job openings. To his surprise he was hired on the spot. In addition to good wages, he would now have complete medical coverage for his family. He and Lynn could not then know that the little boy soon to join them would be born with severe heart defects that meant hundreds of thousands of dollars in medical bills. But the Lord knew, and he responded to the measure of their giving with a like measure of his own.

Jesus said that his meat—what he desired more than daily bread—was to do the will of his Father (John 4:34). His kind of joy may be ours in this special way month by month. We meet our hunger for righteousness with a quiet abstinence from food, a heart full of prayer, and a pocket full of generosity. "The man or woman who will do this will be prospered and blessed," testified Samuel O. Bennion.[63] Our generosity stirs the generosity of heaven.

21.
THE STEADYING ORDINANCES OF THE TEMPLE

I know that your lives are busy, that you have much to do, but I make you a promise that if you will go to the House of the Lord, you will be blessed; life will be better for you. Please, please my beloved brothers and sisters, avail yourselves of the great opportunity to go to the Lord's House.

—Gordon B. Hinckley[64]

How can you tell which one is the quarterback?" the girl asked. The boy sitting next to her pointed down to the player with number 16 on his jersey. "The guy about to throw the ball," he yelled above the shouting crowd. "Ah, yes. The safe one," she nodded with a smile. Her companion looked at her. "The safe one?" he asked. "Sure," she answered. "He just stands there while everyone's running around. He acts so safe, like he can't ever get hurt."

The quarterback is safest when he works calmly, which is also true for the harried soldier, the traffic officer, or even the fry cook. But where will we learn to be calm for our work in the latter-day trenches? In the Lord's house.

By the hand of temple officiators, the Lord stretches toward us and touches us. Otherwise we would feel no edifying and calming power (D&C 88:50). Robert D. Hales declared, "The steadying arm of the Lord reaches us through the ordinances of His holy temples."[65]

Temple workers come and go, but the Lord is ever there. *He* is the one who meets with us at the altars. The ordinances are his, sponsored by his Church in his precise way. He takes it all personally (Mosiah 26:21–24). It is with him that we exchange promises. His protections are placed upon us by his words and his hand (D&C 36:2).

Boyd K. Packer assures us that "there is such a thing as having pure intelligence poured into the mind." He connects this privilege to the temple. "In the temple, the mediation and contemplation that comes from a quietly observed reverence frequently results in such a pouring-in of intelligence and spiritual learning."[66]

That peculiar and sweet cycle, in which reverence paves the way for revelation and revelation inspires yet deeper reverence, is prominent in the house of the Lord. Going there is like ascending a watchtower to obtain a commanding view of our lives (D&C 101:44–48). "Prayers are answered, revelation occurs, and instruction by the Spirit takes place in the holy temples of the Lord," said Ezra Taft Benson.[67]

The ordinances are neither pompous nor trite, neither obscure nor commonplace, for the God of the ordinances is none of these things. The steadying dignity, the majesty and warmth, the simplicity and depth, the positive and promising view of present and future are infused into the temple from the God of the temple. Those characteristics also seep into the reverent and attentive guests. The guests then depart to other duties and schedules, but the calm stays with them and they feel safe.

22.
Joy in Living

Suffering has its place in the scheme of things. It serves a purpose even though the sufferer may be entirely free from the taint of sin. . . . Among the gentlest and sweetest souls are sometimes found those who suffer much. A person that accepts his lot, does his best, loving both God and man, is a success and will experience a joy in living.
—Joseph F. Merrill[68]

Is it possible? Can there be suffering and happiness in the same person? Of course. The best heroes often partake of both simultaneously. "Whatever the storms we are facing personally," declared Robert D. Hales, "joy can be ours now."[69] The model for all heroes, our great Father, knows the full range of joy and sorrow (Moses 7:28). Mortality trains us in this pattern.

While suffering both pain and depression in Liberty Jail, Joseph Smith was blessed, invited, encouraged, even commanded, in these words: "Peace be unto thy soul" (D&C 121:7). How was he to be at peace while sorrowing? By understanding the truth-consoling things about the present and glorious things about the future (D&C 121:8–9, 25–29, 45–46).

Life may be sweet and sour. Mortality supplies the sour part. The other part of the recipe must come from us voluntarily, from our firm response to the assurances of God. Ezra Taft Benson, who underwent so many trials himself, gave this advice: "While you are going through your trial, you can recall your past victories and count the blessings that you do have with a sure hope of greater ones to follow if you are faithful."[70]

Joy can be ours despite troubles. A pebble-sized trouble, stared at too closely, looks as big as a boulder. But no trouble should be allowed to block the light of hope. "When the things you realistically can do to help are done, leave the matter in the hands of the Lord and worry no more," Richard G. Scott advised. "The Lord will take the pebble that fills your vision and cast it down," where it can be seen in perspective with other things. "In time," he promised, "you will feel impressions and know how to give further help."[71] The solution—and the joy—will come more readily if we keep an eye single to what's important.

But can gospel joy survive even in the depths of depression? A severe malfunction in the chemistry or structure of the brain can create a powerful gloom, a daunting current for any swimmer, no matter how brave and strong the swimmer would be in still waters. There is One who sees below the surface. Our struggle against the rushing surge of depression is beautiful to him. He knows that a world already lone and dreary is more so for the depressed person. He hopes we will keep swimming in the direction of joy—taking every possible step to replace the loneliness with fellowship and to drive the dreariness away with every kind of wholesome cheer.

"There are times," said Ezra Taft Benson, "when you simply have to righteously hang on and outlast the devil."[72] Outlasting the devil in this world empowers us to outlast him forever. Certainty stands in the waves of dark emotion like a rocky land mass rests firm amid the salty foam. If brighter times don't dawn today, they will soon (D&C 121:7). We have joy when we are sure of that.

49

23.
NEARER TO GOD

Every trial a man goes through,
if he is faithful in that trial and
does honor to God and his reli-
gion he has espoused, at the
end of that trial or affliction that
individual is nearer to God,
nearer in regard to the increase
of faith, wisdom, knowledge and
power, and hence is more confi-
dent in calling upon the Lord for
those things he desires.
—Lorenzo Snow[73]

The gospel ensures that our eternal career is mostly luxurious, with only one small sliver of time spent in discomfort. That's good news. However, now happens to be the time for that sliver, which can do more to transform us than luxury could ever do. "Each of us must go through certain experiences to become more like our Savior," said Robert D. Hales.[74]

But ordeals of mortality don't just improve us. As the frightened or injured child suddenly turns from play and reaches up, difficulties urge us upward to our Parent. The faithful are not excused from trials, but they do have this guarantee: each trial will bring them nearer to God. The result, as the Lord said to the suffering Joseph Smith, is that their "confidence shall wax strong in the presence of God" (D&C 121:45). They have more assurance in seeking and beseeching him, sensing that wherever he is, that is where they belong.

When the door of discomfort and pain closes upon us, we can be sure that another door has opened. This new door leads into the private chamber of a quiet, watching God. There he patiently awaits us. We are not required to enter, of course. We can remain alone, doubting, self-absorbed, anguished, restless. But he hopes that, with our aching hearts, we will enter. Should we do so, he will gladly sit with us during our dark hour, watching with attention and affection. When our ordeal is finally ended, the chamber of his presence will have become more than a place to visit, even more than a fortress. We will feel at home there.

When affliction has a softening effect upon us, we are paid handsomely for our trouble. "If your afflictions truly humble you, then you see that you're in a position to have the Holy Ghost whisper to you," Henry B. Eyring pointed out. The problem that humbles us turns out to be a great advantage. Confident before God and in whispering distance of him, we can then be guided through the solution. Under these wonderful conditions, Brother Eyring added, "I promise you that he will always prepare a way for your deliverance."[75] Through it all, we have gained that much more experience with our God—we are better acquainted with him and feel nearer to him.

A pioneer who pulled his handcart across the plains in icy agony looked back and asked, "Am I sorry that I chose to come [with that handcart company in that season]?" His answer was fervent: "No! Neither then nor any minute of my life since. The price we paid to become acquainted with God was a privilege to pay."[76]

24.
THE KEY OF MERCY

*If you do not accuse each other,
God will not accuse you. If you
have no accuser you will enter
heaven, and if you will follow
the revelations and instructions
which God gives you through
me, I will take you into heaven
as my back load. If you will not
accuse me, I will not accuse you.
If you will throw a cloak of charity over my sins, I will over
yours—for charity covereth a
multitude of sins.*

—Joseph Smith[77]

Joseph Smith didn't claim perfection, but to the moment he crossed the veil, he was willing to forgive. We might be willing to follow Joseph through the door of heaven, but if we lack the principle of mercy—the key to heaven's gate—the door remains shut.

Harold B. Lee put the principle simply: "Our salvation rests upon the mercy we show to others." A Christlike leniency toward others is sometimes the one gift we can offer in return for God's utter kindness to us. To refuse that scanty donation to our fellow travelers stops us in our tracks, making our hearts weak and our hopes bleak. To act so is to be blind and arrogant. "Unkind and cruel words," Brother Lee continued, "or wanton acts of cruelty toward man or beast, even though in seeming retaliation, disqualify the perpetrator in his claims for mercy."[78]

When we promote ourselves to the Judge's stand, passing blame and sentence on others, our Father doesn't thank us for "helping" him carry out his difficult and divine role. He disapproves. We have only complicated things. Yet another relationship has been muddled. Yet another offense has been hurled against his laws. Withholding our mercy is a gruesome business.

But what if I was right and that scoundrel over there—that enemy of mine—was wrong? "It doesn't really matter what the issue was," declared Thomas S. Monson. "It cannot and should not be left to injure. Blame keeps wounds open."[79] Of course, if that person has proven to be dangerous, I may have to keep out of his path. But staying at a safe distance is one thing; being tart and vengeful in my own feelings is another.

"Should we even forgive our brother or our enemy before they ask it," Joseph Smith testified (and in this matter he had experience!), "our Heavenly Father would be equally as merciful unto us."[80]

Unkind feelings are what Gordon B. Hinckley calls "the poisonous brew of enmity" boiling in the heart. If we will repent of such feelings, the venom will give way to "the sweet peace of Christ." The change "may not be easy, and it may not come quickly. But," he promised, "if you will seek it with sincerity and cultivate it, it will come."[81]

It is nice to speak kindly. But words alone are but cheap jewelry. Real mercy is active, powerful, ready to do something, as was the Prophet Joseph in his last hour. George Albert Smith said, "Our eternal happiness will be in proportion" not only to our talk and feelings but also "to the way that we devote ourselves to helping others."[82] *Helping* is the language of mercy, and mercy unlocks the door to happiness.

25.
LOYAL TO THE WATERS

In this Church there is a stream of living water that flows from the throne of God. . . . Oh, won't you drink of this living stream? For if you will your souls shall never thirst again.
—Charles A. Callis[83]

The Church is far more than a leadership chart or a building, a block of time or even a meeting machine. It is a sponsor of joys, a public address system for the voice of Christ, a training experience for eternity, a network of eternal friendships, a font of comfort, a shelter for the weary, a river of living water. If we are loyal to the Savior's Church, he quenches our thirst.

Connecting us to the throne of God, channeling that sparkling stream, are prophets and other leaders. To ignore them is to ignore the river itself, and to ignore the Source.

Religious people are generally loyal to ancient prophets, safely buried in the distant past. But a living church presents us with prophets who are very much alive. The test is to accept current messages from human messengers, even when the words aren't verified by outward miracles—and they seldom are (Helaman 8:11–13).

Passing that test, we readily adopt our Father's view as our own private stand, whatever the subject. "I may have my own ideas and opinions," said George Albert Smith, "I may set up my own judgment with reference to things, but I know that when my judgment conflicts with the teachings of those that the Lord has given to us to point the way, I should change my course."[84]

It is easy enough to admit the existence of God, to admire his wonders out there somewhere, and even to be enthralled by a display of his power near at hand. But this kind of faith is only a sterile fascination. It has little to do with our thirst. There is another kind of faith that ensures the daily renewal of our very center. This faith looks upon the work of the Church as vital because that is how Jesus sees it. Those with this faith, the faith of loyalty, love him by loving his Church. "Blessed are they," said John W. Taylor, "whose hearts are to build up the kingdom of God."[85]

Those of loyal faith aren't endlessly starting over again on their testimony. They aren't plagued by weeds creeping in from some previous season of unbelief. They don't agonize over every new question or old complaint. And why not? Because they are less thoughtful or less honest about the truth than the critic? No. In fact, they have pursued the truth to its Source and have then taken honesty to the next level, accepting that Source as their personal and supreme Friend. They love the Church he has carefully put in place for them. They welcome his servants into their lives (Matthew 10:40; John 13:20; D&C 84:36).

In their honesty, they admit that a certain light bids them be loyal. Wholeheartedly, they give their minds. Broadmindedly, they give their hearts.

"Cling to the Church and live its principles," said Gordon B. Hinckley, "and I do not hesitate to promise you that your lives will be happy."[86] The loyal will be happy because, defending and building up the water system, never apologizing for it or forsaking it, they have every right to drink deeply from it.

NOTES

1. John Taylor, in *Journal of Discourses*, 26 vols. (London: Latter-day Saints' Book Depot, 1854–86), 22:321.

2. Richard G. Scott, "Learning to Recognize Answers to Prayer," *Ensign*, November 1989, 31.

3. Boyd K. Packer, in Julie A. Dockstader "'You Are Somebody; You Are Son or Daughter of God,' Graduates Told," *Church News*, 17 June 1995, 11.

4. Gordon B. Hinckley, *Be Thou an Example* (Salt Lake City: Deseret Book, 1981), 84.

5. John A. Widtsoe, "The Articles of Faith," *Improvement Era*, April 1935, 237.

6. Bruce R. McConkie, *Doctrines of the Restoration: Sermons and Writings of Bruce R. McConkie*, ed. Mark L. McConkie (Salt Lake City: Bookcraft, 1989), 262.

7. Joseph F. Smith, *Gospel Doctrine* (Salt Lake City: Deseret Book, 1975), 83.

8. Delbert L. Stapley, in Conference Reports of The Church of Jesus Christ of Latter-day Saints (Salt Lake City: The Church of Jesus Christ of Latter-day Saints, 1898 to present), April 1970, 76.

9. Joseph Smith, *Teachings of the Prophet Joseph Smith*, sel. Joseph Fielding Smith (Salt Lake City: Deseret Book, 1976), 151.

10. Wilford Woodruff, quoted by J. Golden Kimball in Conference Report, April 1924, 70.

11. Gordon B. Hinckley, "Inspirational Thoughts," *Ensign*, August 2000, 2.

12. Joseph Smith, in James E. Faust, *Reach Up for the Light* (Salt Lake City: Deseret Book, 1990), 122.

13. Gordon B. Hinckley, "Inspirational Thoughts," 2.

14. Harold B. Lee, in *Teachings of Presidents of the Church: Harold B. Lee* (Salt Lake City: The Church of Jesus Christ of Latter-day Saints, 2000), 34.

15. Joseph F. Smith, *Gospel Doctrine*, 225.

16. Marion G. Romney, in Conference Report, October 1963, 24.

17. Boyd K. Packer, "'The Standard of Truth Has Been Erected,'" *Ensign*, November 2003, 25.

18. Richard G. Scott, "To Be Free of Heavy Burdens," *Ensign*, November 2002, 88.

19. Spencer W. Kimball, "The Rewards, the Blessings, the Promises," *Ensign*, January 1974, 17.

20. Henry B. Eyring, "An Enduring Testimony of the Mission of the Prophet Joseph," *Ensign*, November 2003, 91.

21. John A. Widtsoe, *Millennial Star*, 93:552–53.

22. J. Reuben Clark Jr., in Henry A. Smith, "Glimpses of June Conference," *Improvement Era*, August 1934, 497.

23. Brigham Young, in *Journal of Discourses*, 5:1–2.

24. Harold B. Lee, in *Teachings of Presidents of the Church: Harold B. Lee*, 67.

25. Ibid., 182–83.

26. Gordon B. Hinckley, "The Light Within You," *Ensign,* May 1995, 99.

27. Bruce R. McConkie, in David Croft, "Spare Time's Rare to Apostle," *Church News,* 24 January 1976, 4.

28. Spencer W. Kimball, *The Miracle of Forgiveness* (Salt Lake City: Bookcraft, 1969), 104–5.

29. Rudger Clawson, in Conference Report, April 1916, 44.

30. Joseph Smith, *Teachings of the Prophet Joseph Smith,* 11–12.

31. J. Golden Kimball, in Conference Report, October 1937, 33.

32. Ezra Taft Benson, "A Sacred Responsibility," *Ensign,* May 1986, 77–78.

33. Joseph Smith, *History of The Church of Jesus Christ of Latter-day Saints,* ed. B. H. Roberts, 2d ed. rev., 7 vols. (Salt Lake City: The Church of Jesus Christ of Latter-day Saints, 1932–51), 4:461.

34. Ibid.

35. Ezra Taft Benson, "Jesus Christ—Gifts and Expectations," *New Era,* May 1975, 19.

36. Gordon B. Hinckley, *Faith: The Essence of True Religion* (Salt Lake City: Deseret Book, 1989), 64.

37. Brigham Young, *Discourses of Brigham Young,* sel. John A. Widtsoe (Salt Lake City: Deseret Book, 1966), 269.

38. Richard G. Scott, "Finding Happiness," *Brigham Young University 1996–97 Speeches* (Provo, Utah: BYU Publications and Graphics, 1997), 362.

39. Brigham Young, in *Journal of Discourses,* 2:256.

40. David O. McKay, *Pathways to Happiness,* comp. Llewelyn R. McKay (Salt Lake City: Bookcraft, 1957), 295.

41. Brigham Young, in *Journal of Discourses,* 19:220.

42. Ibid., 2:9.

43. Joseph Smith, *Teachings of the Prophet Joseph Smith,* 256.

44. Joseph F. Smith, *Gospel Doctrine,* 7–8.

45. Joseph Smith, *Teachings of the Prophet Joseph Smith,* 255.

46. Heber J. Grant, in *Collected Discourses,* comp. Brian H. Stuy, 5 vols. (Burbank, Calif.: B.H.S. Publishing, 1987–92), 3:191–92.

47. Joseph Smith, *Teachings of the Prophet Joseph Smith,* 51.

48. The First Presidency, in Conference Report, October 1942, 11–12.

49. Joseph F. Smith, *Gospel Doctrine,* 274.

50. David O. McKay, "Some Essentials of a Permanent Marriage," *Improvement Era,* July 1955, 493.

51. Neal A. Maxwell, "The Seventh Commandment: A Shield," *Ensign,* November 2001, 78.

52. Gordon B. Hinckley, "'Till We Meet Again,'" *Ensign,* November 2001, 90.

53. Spencer W. Kimball, *The Miracle of Forgiveness,* 104–5.

54. David O. McKay, "Some Essentials of a Permanent Marriage," 493.

55. Spencer W. Kimball, *The Teachings of Spencer W. Kimball,* ed. Edward L. Kimball (Salt Lake City: Bookcraft, 1982), 215–16.

56. Ibid., 218.

57. Joseph Fielding Smith, in Conference Report, April 1957, 62.

58. Heber J. Grant, *Gospel Standards*, ed. G. Homer Durham (Salt Lake City: Bookcraft, 1998), 59.

59. Dallin H. Oaks, "Repentance and Change," *Ensign*, November 2003, 40.

60. Melvin J. Ballard, *Millennial Star*, 94:503.

61. Howard W. Hunter, *The Teachings of Howard W. Hunter*, ed. Clyde J. Williams (Salt Lake City: Deseret Book, 2002), 109.

62. Spencer W. Kimball, "Welfare Services: The Gospel in Action," *Ensign*, November 1977, 78–79.

63. Samuel O. Bennion, in Conference Report, October 1907, 114.

64. Gordon B. Hinckley, in "Prophet Visits South America," *Church News*, 16 November 1996, 4.

65. Robert D. Hales, "Faith through Tribulation Brings Peace and Joy," *Ensign*, May 2003, 17.

66. Boyd K. Packer, *The Holy Temple* (Salt Lake City: Bookcraft, 1980), 79.

67. Ezra Taft Benson, *The Teachings of Ezra Taft Benson* (Salt Lake City: Bookcraft, 1988), 179.

68. Joseph F. Merrill, *Millennial Star*, 96:8–9.

69. Robert D. Hales, "Faith through Tribulation Brings Peace and Joy," 18.

70. Ezra Taft Benson, "Do Not Despair," *Ensign*, November 1974, 67.

71. Richard G. Scott, "To Help A Loved One in Need," *Ensign*, April 1988, 60.

72. Ezra Taft Benson, *The Teachings of Ezra Taft Benson*, 396.

73. Lorenzo Snow, in *Collected Discourses*, 1:90–91.

74. Robert D. Hales, "Faith through Tribulation Brings Peace and Joy," 17.

75. Henry B. Eyring, *To Draw Closer to God* (Salt Lake City: Deseret Book, 1997), 86–87.

76. Story retold by David O. McKay in "Pioneer Women," *Relief Society Magazine*, January 1948, 8.

77. Joseph Smith, *History of the Church*, 4:445.

78. Harold B. Lee, *Decisions for Successful Living* (Salt Lake City: Deseret Book, 1973), 58–59.

79. Thomas S. Monson, "Hidden Wedges," *Ensign*, May 2002, 19

80. Joseph Smith, in *Wilford Woodruff's Journal*, ed. Scott G. Kenney, 9 vols. (Midvale, Utah: Signature Books, 1983), 1:342–43.

81. Gordon B. Hinckley, "'Of You It Is Required to Forgive,'" *Ensign*, June 1991, 2, 5.

82. George Albert Smith, in Conference Report, October 1931, 71.

83. Charles A. Callis, in Conference Report, October 1931, 67–68.

84. George Albert Smith, in Conference Report, April 1937, 33.

85. John W. Taylor, in Conference Report, October 1900, 59.

86. Gordon B. Hinckley, *Teachings of Gordon B. Hinckley* (Salt Lake City: Deseret Book, 1997), 116.

Part B
Promises for the Family

The greatest joys of true married life can be continued. The most beautiful relationships of parents and children can be made permanent, . . . but this will never fall into place of its own accord. —Spencer W. Kimball[1]

Just as a tree needs steady care to bring forth the sweetest fruit, beautiful relationships don't just happen. It isn't enough to make one great effort on one special occasion. Several laws must be lived day after day. We now consider twenty-five promises that contribute to the grand promise of family happiness.

26.
A SUPREME ACT OF FAITH

We, the First Presidency and the Council of the Twelve Apostles of The Church of Jesus Christ of Latter-day Saints, solemnly proclaim that marriage between a man and a woman is ordained of God and that the family is central to the Creator's plan for the eternal destiny of His children.

—The First Presidency and Council of the Twelve Apostles[2]

Not long ago society was indifferent toward the family. It was common to wonder: *Should I keep my family small? Should I bring any children into this world? Is a family worth it? Should I even marry?* But recently the tone of the world has changed from apathy to hostility. The personal decisions that once required average faith now require supreme faith.

Against the background of more and more despairing questions, the prophets seem to answer with ever-greater clarity. "Only five times in the history of the Church have the First Presidency and the Quorum of the Twelve Apostles felt it necessary to make a proclamation to the world on any subject," M. Russell Ballard pointed out.[3] The timing of the Proclamation on the Family was no accident. In the din and heat of the last great battle, it is a call to the wise and ancient plan.

Eternal beings such as you and I can reach the towering heights of happiness but in only one way: We must gather into permanent families. This way is perfect. It will never change. When we were at our best—informed and unhurried premortal sages—we voted in favor of it. The Father's plan became ours, encased in the heavenly titanium of solemn agreements. It holds the promise of total fulfillment.

If the world forsakes and deserts the basics, God will stand firm. He refuses to reduce our eternal opportunities even a little. No new council has been held in the heavens to revise the plan. The only change is that a very old war is reaching a new pitch and is inflicting new wounds. The old champions, toe to toe with the evil one again, must trust the plan and its Author as before.

Such a champion was Ray. He was widely known for visiting and relating easily with anyone, including those who were down and out. Few people realized that he knew about the down and out life from his own experience. The first part of Ray's life had been troubled with various addictions, and his frequent visits to jail were mandatory, not voluntary. The gospel came along and he changed completely. The biggest step for Ray was giving himself to family life and deciding whether to go back to his wife and embrace his imperfect children. He feared the relationships that at one time had been painful.

"But I went back and threw myself into it because that's what the Lord wanted," he said. "And I told myself, if family life didn't turn out to be all that rewarding, I'd stay with it anyway. It was the Lord's program."

Ray's only reason to think he could succeed at home was his faith that we were all created to succeed there. He became a family man and never looked back. The most memorable thing about Ray was his affection for his wife and children. When they were near, he simply glowed. Before his recent death, he was one of the happiest men in the world.

27.
THE SACRED SECRET

If you are reverent and prayerful and obedient, the day will come when there will be revealed to you why the God of heaven has commanded us to address him as Father, and the Lord of the Universe as Son. . . . The great plan of happiness (see Alma 42:8, 10) revealed to prophets is the plan for a happy family. It is the love story between husband and wife, parents and children, that renews itself through the ages.

—Boyd K. Packer[+]

Adventure stories sometimes tell of secret passages that can be entered through a plain and unlikely wall into a special corridor, leading to refuge or paradise. That is how it is with family. When we consider that family life is so down-to-earth, we may be surprised that it reaches to the highest heaven. In fact, most of mankind would be shocked at this passage to glory. To share common life in a common space with common people is to be immersed in the basics of emotional and physical survival and to sometimes face the stern realities of mortal need. Mortal problems of illness, unhappiness, sin, and death always hover near at hand.

Family life is so distinctly humble and humbling that uninspired creeds have even looked upon it as unworthy. Without prophets, mankind has sometimes thought that difficult means degrading and that ordinary means petty. But ordinary family life here is patterned after the splendid origins from which we came. Its difficulties groom us for glorious destinations ahead.

David O. McKay said, "I picture

heaven as a continuation of the ideal home."[5] The ideal home is not a prize easily gained. A family may work for years to that end, but generations may pass before all of the finest traditions and reflexes finally come together in one earthly home. If we work at this quest heartily in this life, we will be able to continue at it in the next.

On another occasion, David O. McKay said, "One should make it his highest ambition to build an ideal home. Make home your hobby, for, if anyone makes a loving home with all his heart, he can never miss heaven."[6] He was not only announcing a promise but also sharing an important secret. We will probably not have a great home until this quest becomes our hobby—something we think about and care about when nobody is watching, something that gets our spare time, our spare money, and our unsparing effort.

The ideal home emerges only after it becomes our passion in life, our superlative mission. We make home our pearl of great price when we give all we can to down-to-earth domestic duties and to down-to-earth relationships in order to make them work. Only when we have paid that price will we discover the pearl hidden in that briny and homely shell.

Then we will take another step forward in our understanding of God. We will see that he is "The Father" because his quest, the everlasting hobby to which he gives everything, is the blessing of his imperfect children. When we understand him, we will know how it is that home can be heaven. When we return to him, we will discover that heaven is home.

28.
WORTH OUR BEST EFFORT

I have thought many a time that if I labored until I was as old as Methuselah and by that means could have my family dwell with me in glory in the eternal worlds, it would pay me for all the pain and suffering I could endure in this world.
—Wilford Woodruff [7]

Wilford Woodruff knew his subject. He knew of the difficulties, and he knew of the waiting blessings. The promise is that family joys will be more than worth our patient family labors.

It was late on a cold, clear night in the spring of 1996. Jerry slowly pulled into the driveway of his home, nestled in a community high in the Sierra Madre Mountains. "How do I ever survive Wednesdays?" he wondered. The long commute to an early morning faculty meeting, a full day of classes, a dinnerless evening in orchestra rehearsals, and the long commute home.

On the way into the house, he was startled to see his neighbor out on the lawn next door with a telescope aimed at the sky. Bert taught science at the same small college where Jerry taught music, and Jerry now remembered that they had both left at about the same time that morning.

"Hey, a little late for that isn't it?" Jerry called out. "Aren't you as tired as I am?" Not taking his gaze from the sky, Bert answered, "Doesn't matter how tired you are. Come over here and look at this."

Oh boy. I hope this doesn't take long, Jerry thought. "All right," he said out loud. "What've you got going this time, Mr. Scientist?"

"The chance of a lifetime, that's what. You don't even need the telescope for this," Bert said, pointing up at a part of the star-speckled sky, framed by two large pine trees on the other side of his house. Jerry joined Bert, looked up, and froze. It seemed unreal—a great, almost motionless streak of shimmering white, tinted with emerald green on the lower end where it was brightest, with hints of blue in the long tail that extended up the sky at an arching angle.

"It's a comet called Hyakutake," Bert said softly, his own eyes still riveted. "Worth staying up for after all, isn't it?" Jerry still could not speak, so Bert added, "They say it'll be another forty thousand years before it comes around again." Jerry finally went into his house but only to wake his wife and children so that they could enjoy this rare celestial event with him.

Some things, rare and wonderful, are worth any effort. For example, the opportunity to create a celestial family is so rare that it comes once in all eternity—not before, not again, and not every forty thousand years. Thus, in a plea to every home, the First Presidency said, "We call upon parents to devote their best efforts to the teaching and rearing of their children." Why the urgency? Why call for our maximum best? Because "the home is the basis of a righteous life, and no instrumentality can take its place."[8]

If I am a parent or husband or wife, no previous moment compares to the one now in my grasp. No career—political, medical, educational, or artistic—has such leverage for setting eternal things in motion. If we open our eyes, we see that this mortal chance at family privileges is a rare celestial opportunity.

29.

WE CAN BLESS THE WORLD AT HOME

Joseph Smith taught that the family circle is the foundation of exaltation and that its projection into eternity is heaven itself. He sanctified the association of loved ones. He made the father a priest and the mother a priestess in the temple of the home. If his glorious interpretation of this divine institution could have general application, the ills of society would be cured and the brotherhood of mankind established.

—Stephen L Richards[9]

From the restored gospel we learn that the home is much more than a wholesome headquarters. It is a temple, grooming us for exaltation. Mothers are more than blessed caregivers, and fathers are more than kindly protectors. They are eternal queens and kings in the making. Homes are holy, families are forever, children are everlasting friends, and chastity is crucial.

Taking the classic view to another level, the prophets offer us a glorious interpretation of the family. That glorious interpretation—to understand Christ's gospel as radiated by righteous homes—is the one hope for an inept world caught in a sad spiral.

The matter of gender offers one illustration. To fully understand the sacred roles of man and woman is to dwell safely in a fortress of solid truth while staggering confusion reigns outside its walls. "A correct understanding of the divinely appointed roles of men and women," the First Presidency assured us, "will fortify all against sinful practices."[10]

To fully understand, people must see. At this hour of history, the

Church has before it the greatest task ever undertaken in the whole story of mankind. We are to reach every soul of mankind with our message. In doing so, we are to be perfectly understandable as well as edifying—inspiring, encouraging, and inviting. With the right visual aid, we can do that.

Attended by the Holy Ghost, the most clarifying and edifying teaching tool, we understand that the most effective statement we will make about Christ will be our families. Before or after they have heard our message, the people of every nation must be able to look at our homes in order to grasp what we are saying.

"Our success, individually and as a Church," announced Spencer W. Kimball, "will largely be determined by how faithfully we focus on living the gospel in the home." He then clarified where the programs and organizations of the Church fit into our message: "Priesthood quorums and auxiliary organizations, even wards and stakes, exist primarily to help members live the gospel in the home. . . . I repeat that our success, individually and as a Church, will largely [depend on] how faithfully we focus on living the gospel in the home."[11]

Most people, when they hear the truth, need something more than the information. The truth is true only when it is understandable, visible, and translated into life. That is where we come in. That is where our lives, real and tangible in gospel-centered homes, come in.

"We have no choice . . . but to continue to hold up the ideal of the Latter-day Saint family. . . . We cannot set aside this standard, because so many other things depend upon it."[12] The whole world depends on it.

30.
HONORING THE FUTURE

See that you honor the parents of your children. Give them clean bodies. Prepare yourselves that you can go to the temple and be married in the temple, and take the covenants that you make there. I want to promise you that if you will do that you will have joy, you will have the respect and the confidence of the people with whom you associate, you will be successful in life, you will have a good family, and you will be able to take that family back into the presence of our Heavenly Father.
—Nathan Eldon Tanner[13]

When N. Eldon Tanner asked us to honor the parents of our own children, he was asking that we honor ourselves, that we be good stewards of our own souls. But he was also pointing to other souls—future family members—whose future is affected by our present. Every child should be born into clean family ties, received into clean hands, loved by clean hearts. Every parent should have promises in place, with each other and with God. Every home should be built under the beautiful blue sky of the covenant.

It begins before the birth of children and before marriage, in the beliefs of childhood and the decisions of youth. The best outcomes are, like all other outcomes, lawful. They don't just pop into existence at the wave of a magic wand. The good things Brother Tanner listed—success in life and family—grow out of preparation. We don't have to know precious loved ones yet in order to start giving them every advantage.

Or, by contrast, we could live for the moment only. Our lives could crumble away behind our heels, and we could revel in the passing now and lose title to the future. How different that beast-like style would be from the fully human and humane way: a life that remembers the past and reverences the future, a story always building, preparing for newer and more privileged adventures, sealed to the fellowship of yet further loved ones. God has ordained that this approach—being considerate of what lies ahead—bring the finest joys. This manner of life fits perfectly with the laws of family happiness.

A simple example is how chastity during certain years can profoundly influence the decades that follow. David O. McKay repeatedly taught, "Chastity, not indulgence, during the premarital years is the source of harmony and happiness in the home."[14] For a mighty prophet to announce that chastity is the very source of a fulfilling home life is nothing short of revelation. It is worth serious thought for every person on earth. It presents us with a key. To ignore that key is folly for the individual and ruin for society. Glorious is the destiny of those who honor the future.

The prophets warn us to give no heed to selfish desires (1 Nephi 8:33–34; Jacob 1:8; Alma 39:9; D&C 20:22). Jesus set the pattern when he found the instrument of his own death—a cross—lying upon the ground. Inexpressibly weary, he shouldered it and pulled it to Golgotha in order to complete his mission (John 19:17). He secured the future by bearing his cross in the present. Later he counseled all of us to do likewise, such as when lust seeks admission to our hearts (3 Nephi 12:30.) At such moments, we are entrusted with a treasure—the future.

31.
SHARING THE ULTIMATE PROMISE

The whole subject of the marriage relation is not in my reach, nor in any other man's reach on this earth. It is without beginning of days or end of years; it is a hard matter to reach. We can tell some things with regard to it; it lays the foundation for worlds, for angels, and for the Gods; for intelligent beings to be crowned with glory, immortality, and eternal lives. In fact, it is the thread which runs from the beginning to the end of the holy Gospel of salvation.

—Brigham Young[15]

Alongside the infinite atonement, celestial marriage is the infinite opportunity. Jesus offers the ultimate promise, but only to those who keep the ultimate promise—the marriage promise.

We had a vast array of convictions and loves in our premortal home. Those warm and vivid flames are older than the galaxies. They are not extinguished, though a veil dims our recollection of them. Among the most beloved are the promises and laws of family, which only need to be learned and tried in order to become real to us again. The truth about marriage is modest and quiet, but when it takes root in us and we learn to share our life happily, it is white hot, transforming and lasting.

Celestial marriage is unique for the stature, satisfaction, and status it offers.

Stature, the eventual size and power and beauty of our souls, comes in a certain way—a lawful way. To budding souls such as you and me, marriage is necessary to complete our stature, our path to maturation. It is an elevating curriculum, a developmental school. There is no shortcut to the unselfish traits expected of celestial beings, whose role it will always be to share everything. No other staircase leads all the way. And yet, marriage is even more than a staircase.

Marriage is the only possible *satisfaction* of our built-in spiritual and physical hopes and hungers, the only exploration of all the wiring of our creation, the one fulfillment that matches our enormous size. No other well can satisfy all of our thirsts, and yet marriage is even more than this.

Marriage is also necessary to *status*—not mortal status of course, but immortal status. It is a sign of credibility among eternal beings. Only an eternal couple has license to minister fully among the hosts of the universe.

"The lawful association of the sexes is ordained of God, not only as the sole means of race perpetuation," Joseph F. Smith pointed out, "but for the development of the higher faculties and nobler traits of human nature, which the love-inspired companionship of man and woman alone can insure." He even clarified the sacred place of "sexual union," which he said "is lawful in wedlock, and, if participated in with the right intent is honorable and sanctifying."[16]

No other human tie duplicates the challenges, adventures, and delights, the demands, lessons, and stewardships known to husband and wife. The married couple can miss their chance if husband and wife don't work together at this mission. As companions, they work at each other's destiny, upward or downward. To depress, a spouse can nag, demand, accuse, withdraw, or push. To lift, a spouse can learn with and walk beside, defend, please, befriend, and share everything forever.

32.
AN UNSELFISH LITTLE WORLD

When you are married, be fiercely loyal one to another. Selfishness is the great destroyer of happy family life. If you will make your first concern the comfort, the well-being, and the happiness of your companion, sublimating any personal concern to that loftier goal, you will be happy, and your marriage will go on throughout eternity.

—Gordon B. Hinckley[17]

The original meaning of *companion* is someone who shares your bread, who has the common things in common with you. When we represent the Lord, we are to have a companion, but the principle is even broader than that. The lonely path is not happy or healthy or heavenly. We are better if each day finds us being considerate of somebody—even an imperfect somebody!

Though the eye rarely knows it, our imperfect companion is a sibling from the halls of an ancient home, one of our equals in the timeless universe, struggling along for a moment in this unbecoming and time-bound school. My companion is nobler than she seems and will do much better if I am kind and respectful and sustaining. If I will *sublimate* my personal desires—forget my will and focus on the happiness of my companion—I will find happiness after all.

The ultimate companionship, designed for the perfect sharing, is marriage. Each couple is an Adam and Eve, starting their own world—their own special race intended to grow through eternity—complete with culture and ways adopted from the perfect Father. The ingredient that flavors their world is charity. It may be traced to the relationship between the founders—the husband and wife. Their world of forbearance and cheer is a secure and important and real world. It is happy no matter what is going on in the temporary world that surrounds them.

An older man related this story in a priesthood meeting: "When I was young and we had a couple of small children, I was an okay guy, but I didn't see myself very clearly. I didn't realize that I kind of lived for me—selfish is what I'd call it now, looking back. You know, some little adventure was always taking me out the door. Then I had this experience one Saturday morning. I was waiting to get picked up for a game of golf, just sitting in the living room playing with the kids and talking with my wife. The doorbell rang and I stood up to say good-bye. They just looked at me without saying a word.

"As I stood there with my hand on the doorknob, it hit me that this was wrong, all wrong. I told my buddies to go on without me and spent that day with my family, and a lot of other days since. That was a big turning point in my life."

There is a sure promise to unselfish people: happiness. Selfish people don't have that promise (Matthew 10:39). So when do I get my chance to be really unselfish and find real happiness? I can rehearse and practice on all sorts of people. I can even try my reflexes on people I don't know. But the real realm of unselfishness is with the one who lives in the same spot of time and space with me, the one I know all too well, the one with whom I share time and money, the air I breathe, the meals I eat. In the common places and moments with that companion, forgetting myself is not just a rehearsal for the real world. That little world is the real world.

33.
Unity and Power

Speaking generally, a plan or a policy that may be inferior in some respects is more effective, if men are united upon it, than a better plan would be upon which they were divided.

—George Q. Cannon[18]

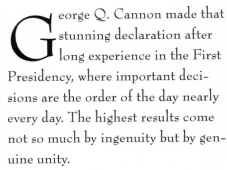

eorge Q. Cannon made that stunning declaration after long experience in the First Presidency, where important decisions are the order of the day nearly every day. The highest results come not so much by ingenuity but by genuine unity.

The Lord hears our conversations but is listening for more than the best opinion. He surveys our projects but watches for more than hard work and good intentions. He cares also about agreement (John 17:11; D&C 27:18; 38:27; 42:3).

In many an unhappy home, people wonder why their most powerful Friend seems so distant. He waits for faith and friendship—the blend of the two great commandments— among those who live in a home. The commandments to love God and to love man can hardly be kept separate, nor can we isolate faith from friendship (Matthew 22:36–40; Mosiah 2:17). Faith in our heavenly Companion fits perfectly with friendship with our earthly one. If we align ourselves with him and with each other, he approves.

Nowhere is this so true as in the matchless little world of a marriage. What we hunger for there is not always what we first suppose. In confused moments we think happiness will come when we finally reach this or that outward goal. But at heart we long to be one (Genesis 2:24). A marriage is grander (and more fun) if we set up life so that we need each other. The way of companions is to divide the work and rely on each other. Thus come our roles in marriage.

Roles are made to fit. They are redemptive, protective, and warm. Our roles make us equal, make us contributors, make us partners, make us meet for each other (Genesis 2:18, 20). Paul gave us a clue to both time and eternity when he wrote, "Neither is the man without the woman, neither the woman without the man, in the Lord" (1 Corinthians 11:11).

Nothing could be more obvious about our Eternal Parents than this: Along with their infinite perfection, they have distinct roles. Womanliness and manliness are like two hands reaching from slightly different places, clasped and inseparable (Genesis 3:16–19). The perfected husband and the perfected wife are not identical to each other or fashioned in the image of each other. Rather, they are in the image of eternal companions (Abraham 4:27).

Husband and wife see through different eyes. This can enlarge their vision or ruin their focus. To keep our eyes single, we can do as George Albert Smith counseled: "Men will not always reason as their wives do and vice versa, but if you will pray together, with a real desire to be united, I can say to you, you will agree on all important matters."[19]

It is no accident that he who has all power is so concerned about unity. He awaits our unity so he can lock arms with us.

34.
THE PROVIDER AND HIS PROVIDER

You are concerned about being able to support a wife and family and provide them with the necessities in these uncertain economic times. Those fears must be replaced with faith. I assure you, brethren, that if you will be industrious, faithfully pay your tithes and offerings, and conscientiously keep the commandments, the Lord will sustain you. Yes, there will be sacrifices required, but you will grow from these and will be a better man for having met them.

—Ezra Taft Benson[20]

Evidently, the story of a faithful husband may not be called "Providing Made Easy." Yet, the provider in the home, with work and wisdom, will be backed by a Provider in Heaven. What is more, he will expand as he works at his calling. There is nothing quite like being fully responsible for the safety and survival of others to help a man grow up. To have no safety net and no bondsman to bail me out may call forth strength and reliability I gain in no other way.

There was a certain woman who planted a young tree at her home. It could have become a shelter, towering high across her grounds and all that would ever be hers. It might have been long-lived and indestructible. But while it was still forming inner tissues, she put tall poles all around it and made supports of rope to thwart the challenges of nature, to soften the tugs of children, and to protect it from distressing passersby. The tree had no need to bear up, no need for heavy fiber.

The wife who enlists in the army of working men, who steps from an eternal role in order to win money for the home, may temporarily be doing the heroic thing. Only she knows how essential is this departure. Only she can discern whether her feminine heart—in the eternal part of her—has gotten too accustomed to filling her husband's mission. And only her husband can tell if he has grown too easy with this altering of things. Unwise patterns, when continued too long, have a way of visiting us with regret in the long run. It is possible for the well-meaning wife to be as those overly protective poles. It is possible to prevent the tree from becoming what it could have been.[21]

Of course, there is such a thing as a one-dimensional husband—one who generates income but gives little time. When Russell M. Nelson declared that "a husband's foremost priority should be the care of his wife," his meaning of the word *care* went beyond the financial.[22] If a man chooses to concentrate on things "more pressing" that the care of his wife, he may someday grieve over that decision. Many important and deserving objects call forth a man's effort. But nothing compares to his unique place in the life of his wife—providing for her security, esteem, and happiness.

The man is the financial provider but also chief friend and emotional comforter. In gospel matters, he does all he can to show the way. As Howard W. Hunter said, he "leads his family in Church participation so they will know the gospel and be under the protection of the covenants and ordinances."[23]

His is not just a job, not just a role. It is a ministry, an eternal mission that never stops getting better, a link with his Provider.

35.
THE HIGHEST PLACE OF HONOR

The true spirit of The Church of Jesus Christ of Latter-day Saints gives to woman the highest place of honor in human life. . . . It is she . . . who wields gradually and constantly the impress of character to childhood and youth, who inspires manhood to noble ambition or entices and ensnares it to defeat and degradation, who makes home a haven of bliss or a den of discontent, who at her best gives to life its sweetest hopes and choicest blessings.
—The First Presidency[24]

This divine assurance—that righteous womanhood outshines and outranks all other human distinctions or offices—can be carved in stone, for it will never change. In this confused world, it should be written not only in male hearts but also in the heart of every woman. Each daughter of God ought to have a testimony of the royal and virtuous possibilities for which she was created. And if this is her place in human life, it should certainly be so in home life too. The men closest to her—husband, son, and father for example—would then esteem her at the summit of their hearts.

When we consider the stunning arts of heaven and earth and remember that we cannot now glimpse the most splendid of them, it is remarkable to think that "woman is God's supreme creation. . . . There is none more beautiful, none more inspiring than a lovely daughter of God who walks in virtue."[25] Even if we look upon mother, wife, and daughter with our better eyes, we do not yet envision the perfect radiance of face and form that will be theirs in the day of resurrection.

Greater yet is the wondrous nurturing power that, if permitted, will expand forever in a woman's giant soul. We only begin to understand this power while she ministers to us here. George Albert Smith testified that "they hold in their hands a power for righteousness and an uplift for a race of people not yet born." (In terms of eternity, we might even say *races* yet unborn!) But there is a caution: "It will take giants all their time to do it."[26]

A woman's influence costs so much of her time that the prophets ask that she not be distracted. For example, Harold B. Lee was alarmed that "women are becoming victims of the speed of modern living." The rushing, pounding pace that the world sets for women shouts down "motherly intuition" and cripples that "marvelous closeness" that means everything to their children.[27]

From the fast lane, golden moments are but a gray blur as they zip past. Opportunities to teach or bond or lift or rejoice soon pass unless the nurturer can ease over to a quiet spot and take the necessary time. A busy life tempts us to haste, but there are fines for speeding: weak ties and famished spirits. The birthright of influence can be traded for a bowl of pottage in the microwave.

Each woman, no matter what her past, is able to make our race greater in her generation. No wonder that the place of highest honor is reserved for her alone.

36.

ALL THE BLESSINGS A HUNDREDFOLD

Not all women in the Church will have an opportunity for marriage and motherhood in mortality. But if those of you in this situation are worthy and endure faithfully, you can be assured of all blessings from a kind and loving Heavenly Father—and I emphasize all blessings. I assure you that if you have to wait even until the next life to be blessed with a choice companion, God will surely compensate you. Time is numbered only to man. God has your eternal perspective in mind.

—Ezra Taft Benson[28]

The second estate affords every chance to embrace our Father's offer. And that estate doesn't end with physical death. It is in the spirit world that the story of salvation unfolds for most of mankind. Even Church members will have much to do when they go to that realm, which is provided for getting straightened out and caught up. Strange would be a plan of salvation that offered less.

The provision for catching up applies as much to marriage as it does to any other gospel privilege. Consider how long the Father has been arranging things for each daughter, how she has been saving up and seeking it for a mighty stretch of pre-mortal time, and how ultimate and precious it will be when she at last gains that much-awaited eternal companion. Such a destiny will not be canceled—though it may be briefly postponed—by whim of fortune or fellow being.

In fact, those who must wait will be compensated "even an hundred fold, yea, more," President Benson declared.[29] All the joys of companionship—the private times and daily talks year upon year, the thousand joint decisions and labors and adventures, all the shared growth—are delayed. And yet they appear on the kind calendars of him who knows all things and who in good time gives all things if we let him (Matthew 21:22; 1 Nephi 9:6; 2 Nephi 9:20; D&C 84:38). The endless cycle of blessings once denied will at last commence and never end. A "hundred fold" is only the beginning.

Until then, there are many schools besides marriage in which to learn the ways of marriage. She who bends her course for that goal can learn of sharing and nurturing in a thousand ways.

As with marriage, so with children. God will not subtract one parental joy from her who could not be a mother in this world. The narrow stewardship to have children here is but an introduction to millennial and eternal maternity. "Many of the sisters grieve because they are not blessed with offspring," Brigham Young acknowledged. Then he made the Lord's promise clear in these words: "You will see the time when you will have millions of children around you. If you are faithful to your covenants, you will be mothers of nations. . . . Be faithful and if you are not blessed with children in this time, you will be hereafter."[30]

Together with all such blessings, the faithful woman, dazzling in unspeakable beauty in the day of her resurrection, will be compensated for her patience and faith. It will be more than a hundred fold.

37.
WELCOMING CHILDREN

"Be fruitful and multiply and replenish the earth." The Lord does not waste words. He meant what he said. . . . Have your family as the Lord intended. Of course, it is expensive, but you will find a way, and besides, it is often those children who grow up with responsibility and hardships who carry on the world's work. . . . Do not limit your family as the world does. . . . Young people, have your family, love them, sacrifice for them, teach them righteousness, and you will be blessed and happy all the days of your eternal lives.
—Spencer W. Kimball [31]

appiness for all the days of eternity is promised those who bid God's offspring to become *theirs,* who invite children in the heavenly home to enter *theirs.* Their motive is far more than duty. As Reed Smoot said, "Every child born into this world has a right to a tender and loving welcome." [32] The eagerness to be a parent is basic to the loving nature of God. It allows us to know his happiness and to live as he lives.

When the gates of life seem locked, a couple may open the door of adoption to express that godly eagerness. Though the route is different, the same blessings follow.

In speaking of a local orphanage, George Albert Smith once counseled the Saints, "If you have no children of your own, . . . reach out your arms and adopt some of these homeless children." Then he promised, "The blessing . . . will not only be that they will rejoice in the growth and development of that child, but that other blessings of our Father will be added to them in proportion to their good works." [33]

The Savior clearly says that he

takes personally what we do unto the least—the most disadvantaged and forgotten—of his people, his needy little ones (Matthew 25:40).

Regardless of the route they use, children don't just fall into the arms of eager and faithful parents by accident. Russell M. Nelson taught that "children of the covenant were designated in the premortal realm."[34] They are select, handpicked volunteers, children of purpose and promise, men and women from heaven, guided carefully to the right arms, here on a mission.

Eve was warned about the discomfort of motherhood, a discomfort not limited to the prelude to birth. Eve was also told that parenthood would increase her size (Genesis 3:16 and footnote 16b). This certainly applies to the growth in character that would come to her and her husband in their family adventures. We, who need so much refinement and growth, just happen to hold the key. We may use it to open the door of life and love to some of our Father's children. If we let them come, he will build us.

He certainly built this planet to supply all the needed ingredients (D&C 49:19; 59:17–19). Reed Smoot declared, "God will provide for the men and women who, willingly and lovingly, bring children into this world and teach them His commandments."[35] The Creator sees to it that we have enough for the children we welcome.

38.
THE ART OF GOD HIMSELF

Now, fathers and mothers, appreciate your children. Don't turn them over to somebody else to train and educate in regard to matters of eternal life. That is your privilege, and it is a privilege. Teach them to pray and walk uprightly before the Lord, and then in time of need they can go to him, and he will answer their prayers. It will be astonishing to you the great happiness that will come into your home that you theretofore have not enjoyed, if you will follow this counsel.

—George Albert Smith[36]

Parental joy comes in proportion to our effort in the parental role. Much as we may trust other people, we have no right to shift to them the destiny of our children. Though others may have time on their hands, it is not their assignment to spend days and years with the souls entrusted to us. Much as we hope the best for others, we are not authorized to delegate to them the joy appointed for us. The greatest tests of our second estate are primarily about loyalty. After loyalty to God and spouse comes the test of being true to our children.

A priesthood leader heard some of the men in his ward say they had to baby-sit their children during an upcoming evening so that their wives could attend a Relief Society meeting. Something about this seemed out of focus, so in a quorum meeting he made this comment: "Brethren, I don't question our willingness to be with our children. But I wonder about this word we use. Baby-sit? Are we the baby-sitters or the fathers of these children? Are we really just a handy person to tend a child for the evening? Or is it our privilege to be there whenever we can and to be their companions for all time and all eternity?"

Artists have been known to give up every comfort, to sacrifice health and even life, for the thrill of creation, the joy of making beauty or meaning out of chaos. For example, works of amazing skill and detail, fashioned from wet sand, adorn popular beaches around the world nowadays. The sand sculptors seem comfortable about the short life of their work, which crumbles under the weather after a few hours or days.

More permanent works—cut into stone, preserved in human literature, transformed into melody, or layered on the best canvas— last only a little longer than sand sculpture when measured against the stretches of eternity, regardless of how rewarding they are to their creators. Other works, however, outlast waves and winds forever.

Parenthood is the ultimate art. We enter at will into the temple of a child's living consciousness. We are authorized to beautify and edify a durable and growing little world. We make lasting impressions on eternal clay while it is still wet. We make a difference that never ends. We build a soul and then, wonder of wonders, that soul becomes our bosom friend in the realms ahead.

The joy in this art may resemble the rewards of other creative labors but on a decidedly higher plane. It dwarfs the enjoyment of composers, authors, and sculptors. The honor and drama and importance of parenthood is worth surrendering all that artists sacrifice and more.

"Of all the joys of life," Gordon B. Hinckley testified, "none other equals that of happy parenthood. . . . To rear children in an atmosphere of love, security, and faith is the most rewarding of all challenges."[37] It is the art of God himself.

39.
INFLUENCE FOR THE LONG RUN

God . . . will not leave us with-
out . . . blessings and inspira-
tion in terms of what we should
say in our families, especially in
those moments when what we
say really matters. He will, if we
treasure up proper things in our
parental minds, give us that
portion we need to respond to
our children. . . . Our children,
who are our real treasures, will
be saved if we will take our rela-
tionships with them seriously
enough to do specific things and
regularize those things in a fam-
ily lifestyle.
—Neal A. Maxwell [38]

Some children, no matter how well they know the gospel, may choose to leave the track and go on a detour through distant hills. Anguished parents watch as the child disappears over the horizon. But the child has not vanished, nor have the childhood memories and premortal longings. The prodigal son, in his far country, cannot outrun the years of warm togetherness. He cannot erase crystalline hours feeling the faith of tender parents. So he uses his power of choice once again, this time to turn his steps homeward on the strength of things remembered (Luke 15:11–32; Proverbs 22:6).

The parent who has a long record of love—and by that love is willing to "regularize" gospel teaching in the home—will someday see that blessed silhouette on the horizon. Prodigal children of such parents will "eventually return again, lest they lose their place in the eternal family circle."[39]

If we cannot save them now, we can love them now and save them later. If we cannot have immediate influence, we at least want a promise of *eventual* influence. We have that promise.

Influence for the long run is the kind that matters. The Master of influence describes his way as "gentleness and meekness." It is the way of all exalted beings, a style in which "sharpness" is rare and brief and serves as the sure prelude to "an increase of love" (D&C 121:41).

Brigham Young said, "It is not by the whip or the rod that we can make obedient children."[40] If harshness doesn't help other human relationships, how can it help the most tender and sensitive ones of all?

But perhaps we are tempted to use harshness because it seems to bring quick results. Those results are fleeting, and they are not really influence. Harshness, said Joseph Smith, "has a tendency to harrow up all the harsh feelings and depress the human mind."[41] In this day of depressed minds, that is a clue and a caution. The Lord's way is the slow way, but it is also the only way.

Joseph F. Smith, despite all of his trials during child-rearing years, managed not only to raise noble children but also to stay close to them. He gave this counsel: "If you wish your children . . . to love the truth and . . . to be . . . united with you . . . prove to them that you love them by your every word or act to them. . . . Speak to them kindly. . . . Use no lash and no violence. . . . You can't do it by unkindness; you cannot do it by driving; our children are like we are; we couldn't be driven; we can't be driven now. . . . Men are not in the habit of being driven; they are not made that way."[42]

Our children cannot be driven because they were carefully designed to steer their own lives. They were made by a Father whose approach is kind and indirect, and who whispers (Isaiah 54:8, 13; 3 Nephi 11:3; D&C 58:26–28). The most influential parents are the ones who most resemble him.

40.
THE
REDEEMING
OF OUR
CHILDREN

It is not uncommon for respon-
sible parents to lose one of their
children, for a time, to influ-
ences over which they have no
control. They agonize over rebel-
lious sons or daughters. They
are puzzled over why they are so
helpless when they have tried so
hard to do what they should. It
is my conviction that those
wicked influences one day will
be overruled.
—Boyd K. Packer[43]

Redemption is the very theme of the gospel. It is all about pulling precious things out of the fire. In other words, the mighty Redeemer saves people and relationships that others, with weaker eyes, consider to be hopeless.

We have faith that Christ can fix what is badly broken. From this absolute trust comes an energy we call hope. It allows us to see past the obvious hardness or weakness or insanity in ourselves and in others. The eye anointed with faith and hope—knowing there comes a time of relief and happiness—gives the heart permission to be of good cheer. Normally, affection for a troubled soul only deepens pain, inspires despair, and prevents peace. But the greater our confidence in the Saving Being, the more positive our hope. In turn, the more calm and patient and steady is our feeling toward the wayward soul.

This way of beholding people is more powerful than typical human love. It "suffereth long, and is kind, . . . beareth all things, believeth all things, hopeth all things, endureth all things." It "never faileth" (Moroni 7:45–46).

"When family members disappoint us," counseled Marvin J. Ashton, "we especially need to learn endurance. As long as we exercise love, patience, and understanding, even when no progress is apparent, we are not failing. We must keep trying."[44]

True followers of Christ are amateur versions of him. They have redemptive kinds of thoughts. They do redemptive things. They are redemptive persons. They never give up. What is more, they are aided by other redemptive beings.

Harold B. Lee reassured us that "there are forces that come into play after parents have done all they can to teach their children." For example, "such a force influenced the younger Alma."[45] The parents of Alma were not put off by his personal sins or by his impudent and rash warfare against the Church. They sorrowed in private but kept the covenant. They did all they could but kept calm. They hoped on until the timing of heaven was right for their son. Forces came into play. Former influences were overruled. The promise to faithful parents was kept through the ministering of an angel (Mosiah 27:8–24; Alma 36:6–21).

Joseph Smith stated the promise clearly: "When a seal is put upon the father and mother"—that is, when they have entered into gospel ordinances and kept their covenants in righteousness—"it secures their posterity, so that they cannot be lost, but will be saved by virtue of the covenant of their father and mother."[46]

The story of young Alma is not an isolated or lawless miracle. Such is the redemptive work of Christ. He starts at the center of the gospel covenant, where faithful parents live.

41.
CHILDREN: OUR YOUNG AGENTS

Each of us is unique. Each child is unique. Just as each of us starts at a different point in the race of life, and just as each of us has different strengths and weaknesses and talents, so each child is blessed with his own special set of characteristics. We must not assume that the Lord will judge the success of one in precisely the same way as another.

—Howard W. Hunter[47]

Some plants and animals are too small to see with the naked eye; some are too big to fit in a warehouse. Some live but a few moments; others easily outlive humans. The substances and sensations, the textures, tastes, tones, and talents that naturally occur in the earth are beyond the width of human grasp. The Creator whose hand displays so much diversity has planted the seeds of variety in his children as well. In setting out the straight path of salvation, he provided a great network of access ramps to the road leading home. For each of our children, no matter how unique, there awaits a specially designed on-ramp.

Our family was reading together from Alma 4. When it was time for our five-year-old to read, I placed her on my lap, looked down at the page, and sighed. Verse 6, a longish one with longish words. *Oh well,* I thought, *we'll get through it.* I read a few words at a time and she repeated them. In the third line, I read, "Have you sufficiently . . ." She imitated the words perfectly. Then came, "retained in remembrance . . ." She repeated again.

The words spoken so carefully, twice now, hung in the air. Thinking that something important was coming, I read on with interest, "the captivity of your fathers?" The little voice echoed with precision. Then the little eyes looked up for an explanation.

We discussed certain ancestors who had embraced the restored gospel. We read more: "his mercy and long-suffering towards them. . . . He has delivered their souls from hell." Somehow it dawned on us that this wasn't just about ancestors. My wife, a person of virtuous life, said that she rejoices in Christ's mercy and long-suffering to *her*. My children were quick to note that *I* needed that mercy more than my wife did.

"But Dad," said our eighteen-year-old, "we're supposed to remember the mercy of Christ to you and Mom because *we* need it. Right?" The room was quiet as I nodded. We read further with new attention, including these words in verse 14: "Have ye spiritually been born of God?" As we were kneeling for our prayer, my wife added this thought: "Parents can't do that for you. Fortunately, that's your private privilege."

In a way, she was teaching our children what Ezekiel said: "The son shall not bear the iniquity of the father, neither shall the father bear the iniquity of the son" (Ezekiel 18:20). Nor, for that matter, can brother or sister, teacher, friend, or bishop. As iniquity is a private burden, faith is a private privilege. It is a wondrous opportunity we would not take from our children. And we could not if we wanted to.

We are the spiritual agents of our children—in their behalf—for a season only. From birth, the clock ticks away at our role. It is our Father's plan and promise that each of his unique children will become responsible, "agents unto themselves" (D&C 29:35, 39; Moses 6:56).

42.
A Ten-Fold Pleasure

Something prevents the husband and the wife from gathering their families, their children, in their household and observing this duty. O, I haven't time to pray this morning. The temptation is great to omit it. I testify unto this congregation that if you will go to your homes . . . and will humbly seek your Father in prayer and in supplication, . . . you will grow and increase and life will become a ten-fold pleasure to you. . . . Try it.

—Brigham Young Jr.[48]

Some families have had a neighbor who admired the children, knew all their names, and became a lifelong friend. It is easy to turn to this neighbor for advice or to borrow a hoe. Our closest and kindest Neighbor is always home, and he is always interested. Joseph Smith once suggested that in prayer, "Be plain and simple, and ask for what you want, just like you would go to a neighbor and say, 'I want to borrow your horse to go to the mill.'"[49]

Spencer W. Kimball gave us a key when he said that "prayer is an armor of protection against temptation."[50] As individuals sin, so do families. Families can have unhealthy habits and combined weaknesses, and family members can complicate each other's sorrows. As individuals need armor, so do whole families. No wonder Brigham Young Jr. warned that a certain influence tempts us to skip our family prayer and to thus miss out on the "ten-fold pleasure" he promised.

Each family is entitled to draw heaven into the home, to rejoice in its friendship and nearness. If family members seek diligently, they will find

(3 Nephi 18:21; D&C 23:6; 88:63). Home need not be a lonely speck; it can be cradled day and night among the hosts of heaven. By prayer we open a curtain.

God doesn't make a show, of course. His closeness is not stark and tangible during the mortal adventure. But by regular family visits to sacred ground, we let the Father fuse his might to the hearts gathered before him. More than any watchful parent, he sees problems before we do. Because of frequent family prayers, he often solves problems without making a fuss. We permit him to lighten burdens and lead us from temptation. Prayer after prayer, we give him our ongoing permission to breathe his peace among us. He is present in his own remarkable way.

Because life can be hard at times, Gordon B. Hinckley counseled: "Pray over your children . . . that they may be shielded from the evils of the world, ... that they may grow in faith and knowledge. . . . Husbands, pray for your wives. . . . Wives, pray for your husbands."[51]

Love leads us to care about the fearsome moments our dear ones may face this hour or this day. Faith leads us to plead for them. Those who pray only for themselves have little grasp of the power of prayer. Unselfish prayer is pleasing to the Lord. He answers it! Consider how any parent feels when one child pleads the cause of another.

A ten-fold pleasure is ours in the safety and goodness of our homes, the wonder of answer after answer from God himself to our little families as the years go by. And a hundred fold greater than that awaits us when our families gather before their often-sought, living Neighbor when the mortal adventure is over.

43.
TRYING THE
TRUTH
TOGETHER

*We as a Church have as a basic
part of our program . . . to conse-
crate one evening a week to sing
together, to instruct one another
in the ways of the Lord, to kneel
together in prayer, there to thank
the Lord for his mercies and to
invoke his blessings upon our
lives, our homes, our labors, our
land. . . . I do not hesitate to
promise you that both you and
your children will become increas-
ingly grateful for the observance
of this practice.*
—Gordon B. Hinckley[52]

Family home evening is an
actual function of our Father's
kingdom. In our private abode,
no matter what it may be, we are
authorized by priesthood and honored
by heaven to hold our little gathering
of Israel. Here we conduct our
Father's business and try on his pure
truth. His work is placed in the hands
of humble parents and untried children and goes forward in modest
holiness. Sometimes, like the stake
president showing up at a ward meeting or social, he may visit.

Those who see home evening as a
waste of time often *truly* waste that
time in some other way. Of course,
"our time" isn't really ours. We had no
hand in creating the minutes we use
up. And yet, those times that the
Creator claims just happen to profit
us more than they profit him. If we
spend them according to his will, the
years will prove the wisdom of our
investment. Of all sacred times, home
evening is like no other. It empowers
our children to walk in pure truth.

Gordon B. Hinckley illustrated
this by a reminiscence: "In 1915
President Joseph F. Smith asked the

people of the Church to have family home evening. My father said we would do so, and so we would warm up the parlor where Mother's grand piano stood and do what the President of the Church had asked.

We were miserable performers as children. We could do all kinds of things together while playing, but for one of us to try to sing a solo before the others was like asking ice cream to stay hard on the kitchen stove. In the beginning, we would laugh and make cute remarks about one another's performance. But our parents persisted. We sang together. We prayed together. We listened quietly while Mother read Bible and Book of Mormon stories. Father told us stories out of his memory. . . .

Out of those simple little meetings, held in the parlor of our old home, came something indescribable and wonderful. Our love for our parents was strengthened. Our love for brothers and sisters was enhanced. Our love for the Lord was increased. An appreciation for simple goodness grew in our hearts. These wonderful things came about because our parents followed the counsel of the President of the Church. I have learned something tremendously significant out of that."[53]

In what other way, from what other meeting, or by what other device could such blessings come to a family? No other success can compensate for a failure to hold home evening. When we council, plan, socialize, learn, and worship together, our children learn to walk in the truth.

44.
IT STARTS WITH THE WORD

I promise you that daily family prayer and scripture study will build within the walls of your home a security and bonding that will enrich your lives and prepare your families to meet the challenges of today and the eternities to come.

—L. Tom Perry[54]

Our discipleship gives us things to do monthly, such as home teaching and visiting teaching. We do other things each week, such as Church meetings and family home evening. But if we ignore the daily things, everything else suffers. Daily immersion in the scriptures is like a nourishing family meal.

Our family will always remember the summer we prepared and ate our meals in a tiny bedroom while we were remodeling the kitchen of our home. Without a stove and refrigerator, the menu was pretty short. Mealtime was so much trouble that we might have decided not to eat at all, but for some reason that idea never occurred to us. Under the worst conditions, you still have to nourish your body if you want it to work. The same is true of the spirit.

Since those days, we have had countless meals in that kitchen. To finish the kitchen and then keep eating in that bare little bedroom, or skip eating altogether, would have been silly. But kitchens aren't the only things that help families eat every day. Good people have put up with all kinds of trouble in order to make the word of the Lord user-friendly and inexpensive for families. Now, in this day of famine, we would be fools to let it just sit (Amos 8:11–13).

The prophets tell us of the "power of the word" and the grand changes that take place when we "receive the word" (Luke 8:13; 2 Nephi 1:26; Jacob 4:9; Alma 5:5; 16:16–17; 4 Nephi 1:30). Henry B. Eyring pointed out that "you and those you love will receive the word of God by obeying it."

The word of the Lord carries a power like nothing else in the world, but that power is released by hearing and then by *obeying* (3 Nephi 14:24). Notice what Elder Eyring said would happen to our families if we not only listened but also *obeyed* the word: "That will allow them to feel His love. . . . When we feel that love we can know that our course in life is approved of God. That is the feast of the delicious fruit described in the Book of Mormon."[55] All this receiving starts with the word.

Every day we can nourish spirits, sooth minds, fill hearts, and renew truth. And every day we can cleanse the air of the dark viruses of discord, confusion, and melancholy that are multiplying in the latter-day world.

It is one thing to know in our minds that our Father loves us but something greater to *feel* that love. It is wonderful to know he is "up there" somewhere but far more wonderful to sense our connection with him down here. Ezra Taft Benson promised blessings to those families that "immerse themselves in the scriptures" daily: "Testimonies will increase. Commitment will be strengthened. Families will be fortified. Personal revelation will flow."[56]

This sacred experience, which costs us nothing but time, is not like anything else we could give our families. And it can be theirs every day.

45.

A SPECIALIZED TOOL FOR THE LATTER DAYS

I feel certain that if, in our homes, parents will read from the Book of Mormon prayerfully and regularly, both by themselves and with their children, the spirit of that great book will come to permeate our homes and all who dwell therein. The spirit of reverence will increase; mutual respect and consideration for each other will grow. . . . Righteousness will increase. Faith, hope, and charity—the pure love of Christ—will abound in our homes and lives, bringing in their wake peace, joy and happiness.
—Marion G. Romney[57]

Scripture can "permeate"—fill, infuse, saturate—a home with harmony, happiness, and hope. It seems too good to be true, but it is true. The Lord actually offers this advantage to every willing latter-day home. The Book of Mormon was given for this purpose—to bless homes.

Comparing private study to family study, Ezra Taft Benson said, "Individual scripture reading is important, but family scripture reading is vital." In these few words, a holy prophet taught us a stunning principle, one we might not have imagined without revelation. But then he added another principle, comparing general scripture study with Book of Mormon study in particular:

"Reading the Book of Mormon together as a family will especially bring increased spirituality into your home and will give both parents and children the power to resist temptation and to have the Holy Ghost as their constant companion. I promise you that the Book of Mormon will change the lives of your family."[58]

Craftsmen have specialized tools

for doing special jobs. You and I might try to tighten the brakes on a car by poking a screwdriver into the wheel housing, but a brake specialist knows that those brakes were designed to be adjusted with a special tool. Our families and the conditions around us in the latter days call for a special tool. To raise our children to their spiritual possibilities without using that carefully designed book would be like trying to shape granite blocks using chisels made of glass and hammers made of clay.

Janice, a single mother, had five interesting children. You would have trouble finding a wider range of personalities and talents in any five people on earth. When the youngest was old enough to ride a bicycle, he mostly preferred to take them apart. The oldest loved playing the violin and didn't mesh with the second oldest, who played the base guitar. None of these had a lot in common with the daughter who started begging to wear makeup at age ten and was fixing her hair whenever she wasn't looking at fashion magazines. And the soccer addict with the crazy sense of humor didn't even look like the others.

"The Book of Mormon didn't make us just alike. It didn't bunch us together," Janice says. "But it bridged our gaps. Every day, it put us all on the same big foundation. We could be there all day long."

Janice's family was experiencing that reverence Marion G. Romney promised. At the flashing of temptation or when you or I might speak unkindly to another or insist on our interest above others, the spirit of the Book of Mormon calls to mind what is really important . . . all day long.

46.
AT HOME WITH THE TEMPLE SPIRIT

Attend the temple on a regular basis. Make sure in your planning that you include a visit to the temple as often as personal circumstances will allow. I promise you that your personal spirituality, relationship with your husband or wife, and family relationships will be blessed and strengthened as you regularly attend the temple.

—Howard W. Hunter[59]

The family is enriched by how we behave in private, how we serve in the Church, and how we worship in the home, but the enrichment needn't stop there. The house of the Lord also has a major part to play in our homes. It cleanses, soothes, and vitalizes with its own special oil. The temple of God invites us and appoints us to keep progressing until we become like him. And it endows us with power to do so (D&C 105:11–12). There is a big difference between the home that is networked with the temple by service "as often as personal circumstances will allow" and the home that is orphaned from its mother home.

A house can be like a mirror, reflecting the spirit of whoever dwells there. The temple, because it really is the house of the Lord, is different from any other dwelling on earth. It mirrors his presence and power. And yet, our houses can be connected with the Lord's. Thus, John A. Widtsoe testified, "The path from the temple to the home of man is divinely brilliant. Every home penetrated by the temple spirit enlightens, cheers, and comforts every member of the household. The peace we covet is found in such homes."[60]

It is a special mercy that blesses *every* member of the family, even the one who may not seem to care. All of us covet the peace of Christ somewhere in our heart. Living in the home of a faithful patron of the temple is a boon that can eventually draw the careless person to God.

Elder Widtsoe pointed out that "whoever seeks to help those on the other side receives help in return in all the affairs of life." Can our temple labors actually benefit our temporal work? Can the temple's lively powers affect our daily life and even our livelihood? "I can think of no better preparation for one's labor on the farm, in the office, wherever it may be, than to spend a few hours in the temple, to partake of its spirit and to give oneself unselfishly for the benefit of those who have gone beyond the veil."[61] The temple radiates. It sends blessings to both sides of the veil.

In modern revelation, the Lord likened his house to a tower (D&C 101:41–45). It is a perfect comparison. Many of us have gone to the temple perplexed by some problem or decision and while there received even more than a prompting or even an answer. We received a grander view. We saw as we had not seen before. We understood the situation afresh because we could see so far.

In the Lord's high tower, we are not distracted by the stresses and confusion below. We are presented only with those things that matter forever. The landscape stretches in every direction.

What does it take to get ourselves up that tower? The price is twofold. First, we live an elevated life, worthy of those who can be trusted with the towering view. And second, we take time to go there and calmly consider that view. It is a wonderful price to pay.

47.
A Little Heaven on Earth

Happiness in family life is most likely to be achieved when founded upon the teachings of the Lord Jesus Christ. Successful marriages and families are established and maintained on principles of faith, prayer, repentance, forgiveness, respect, love, compassion, work, and wholesome recreational activities.

—The First Presidency and Council of the Twelve Apostles[62]

Great results come by a combination of causes. That lesson is everywhere. A living tree needs more than sunshine, a child needs more than food, a runner needs more than feet, and a house needs more than nails. It even takes more than love alone to build a happy home. If heaven could come from a single ingredient, God would not have created a "great plan of happiness" (Alma 42:8). In the realms of reality, whether physical or spiritual, great things come of many ingredients. Nothing is more clearly physical *and* spiritual than family happiness.

Thus, present-day prophets proclaim the need for more than faith; there must be prayer in the home of faith. They call for repentance, but they also list forgiveness. They include the tenderness of compassion and the dignity of respect alongside love. When they list work, they add recreation as well. Through his servants, God pleads for balance. This full range of essentials, this wholeness at home, creates a wonderful spirit. But it does not come without private pondering, sincere conversation, regular planning, kind restraint, unselfish effort, and harmony with the prophets (D&C 121:41–45).

As our leaders said, it is a matter of basing home life on the teachings of Jesus Christ—all of them. The spirit of a home is no accident.

To believe or suppose there is a God and leave it at that is a convenient and common sort of faith. It has little influence on the lives lived in the home, and it produces little spirit there. A strong spirit of goodness—a radiance that edifies those who visit, that braces and encourages each member of the household, that whispers there is more to life than what we see—comes from another kind of faith. This other faith accepts every word of Christ as a guideline for doing. This faith brings the prophets home. It practices what they preach.

A man named Amulek honored and sustained the prophet Alma in every way he could and at every expense, even inviting him into his home. Amulek later testified that the prophet "hath blessed mine house, he hath blessed me, and my women, and my children, and my father and my kinsfolk; yea, even all my kindred hath he blessed, and the blessing of the Lord hath rested upon us" (Alma 10:11; see also D&C 75:19). To welcome a prophet into the home always brings the peace of God as well, whether the prophet is physically present or not.

Heeding the proclamation of modern prophets makes them, and the spirit that inspires them, part of our families. "If you will follow the admonitions of the Lord and heed the counsel of His chosen servants in their callings as prophets, seers and revelators," declared Ezra Taft Benson, "I promise you that . . . each of our homes may veritably become a little heaven on earth."[63]

48.
THE CULTURE OF HEAVEN AT HOME

All should work together to make home a place where we love to be, a place of listening and learning, a place where each member can find mutual love, support, appreciation, and encouragement. . . . Our success, individually and as a Church, will largely [depend on] how faithfully we focus on living the gospel in the home.

—Spencer W. Kimball [64]

Every home has its own culture—a little world of views and traditions, economy and calendar, mission and habits, fun and work. That culture can be tragic or glorious—or something in between. Only those who live in a home can create or change its culture. Our success and even the success of the Church, according to Spencer W. Kimball, depend on what we create—the culture we make—at home.

J. Reuben Clark Jr. declared this principle when he said, "The home is the basis of a righteous life and no other instrumentality can take its place nor fulfill its essential functions."[65]

The culture of heaven comes by really believing what God believes about daily life. He has a perfect outlook on everything: hard work, modesty and morality, dignity and cleanliness, friendships (especially friendships between family members), and even our entertainment.

Members of one family actually put part of their culture in writing. They were struck by these words of

M. Russell Ballard in general conference: "The choices we make in media can be symbolic of the choices we make in life. . . . If we do not make good choices, the media can devastate our families."[66] The family decided on their own policy about movies: "We don't mind turning off a movie partway through. Even if the story is interesting or the acting is great, if we don't think Elder Ballard would approve, we will push stop and rewind it. Movies are not our bosses." That is culture.

Surrounded by the world's culture of contention, we need to protect the friendships in our homes. Here is one glimpse of the culture of heaven we can create: "On March 25, 1988, my friend and I attended a session at the Jordan River Temple. . . . The temple session started slightly late due to the arrival of President Ezra Taft Benson and his wife, Flora. I can still see the tender care of love he showered on his beloved as they were going through this session. . . . As I entered the celestial room, I shook hands with Sister Benson and then President Benson. President Benson asked me if I was getting married in the near future. I answered, 'Yes, sir, tomorrow.'

"President Benson then told me: 'Always treat your wife as if you were in the presence of the Lord. And remember, if you ever feel like having an argument, stop and ask yourself if it is worth destroying your marriage over. My wife and I have never had an argument in all of our years.'"[67]

We have the culture of heaven when we live as if we were in the presence of the Lord. If we so live, that is just where we will be.

49.
THE POWER AND JOY OF KINDNESS

Nothing is so much calculated to lead people to forsake sin as to take them by the hand, and watch over them with tenderness. When persons manifest the least kindness and love to me, O what power it has over my mind.
—Joseph Smith[68]

The most influential man to live on earth in many centuries knew what he was talking about. The way to influence others is the tender hand of fellowship—sincere kindness.

The family is the best place for holding hands, never labeling or belittling, never withdrawing fellowship. If we are committed to Christ's way of interacting—the way of the prophets, the way of heaven—we will be surprised at how much use the Lord can get out of us and at how satisfying our relationships will be. Those who don't take his way will taste regret.

Unkindness and confrontation are guaranteed to shut off interest, dull listening ears, and weaken respect. Family members may somehow tolerate us in our abruptness, loudness, or aggression, but toleration alone doesn't fill a heart with affection and loyalty.

We cannot enter the courts of exaltation alone. So why not slow down and walk side by side with my companion, my child, or my parent? Hand in hand is what we all need to make our changes. As long as two of us are willing, we can change if only we have each other.

Occasionally people think they have "fallen out of love" with their spouse. Something about that sounds odd, doesn't it? One day a young friend came to share that very worry. I asked, "Do you have other troubles like this? You know, things falling out of your pocket all the time or tools falling out of the trunk of your car, or maybe food falling out of your spoon?" He chuckled and said he didn't have troubles like that because he "followed" the rules of pockets and trunks and spoons.

We decided that there must be some rules for holding on to love. We came up with *attention, respect,* and *tenderness.* He wrote them down, looked again, and said, "Hey, that spells a-r-t, doesn't it?" We had accidentally outlined an art—the art of kindness.

Attention, respect, and tenderness don't work if they are merely prizes we hand out to those who are nice to us (Matthew 5:46). What if we gave food to our children only if they were good? We have all met children who would starve under such a system. Meals are a part of life, as when God sends rain and sunlight on all people (Matthew 5:45). Kindness is basic to sanity in both giver and receiver. To withhold it only makes the soul more ill.

Family ought to be world headquarters for kindness. Marriage is where kindness is learned most perfectly and expressed in all its fulness. Therefore, what could trouble the heart of prophets? How might we drive them to sorrow? Gordon B. Hinckley answered in general conference: "We are deeply concerned over the quality of the lives of our people as husbands and wives and as parents and children. There is too much of criticism and faultfinding with anger and raised voices."[69]

The harsh habit of freely criticizing is nothing short of a deadly curse. It is Satan's ticket right into the home. Kindness drives him out of the home and draws heaven in.

50.

LEAVING A PRECIOUS RECORD

I promise you that if you will keep your journals and records and write your personal histories, they will indeed be a source of great inspiration to your families, your children, your grandchildren, and others, on through the generations. . . . As our posterity read of our life's experiences, they too will come to know and love us. And in that glorious day when our families are together in the eternities, we will already be acquainted.
—Spencer W. Kimball [70]

We have the privilege of teaching our descendants what is important. They will take us seriously, just as we heed those who came long before us. Our words, in the eyes of people living centuries from now, people who will consider us ancestors, will have enormous weight. But we can't put off until tomorrow saying our piece to them. Today is the ancient yesterday they will savor.

Therefore, Spencer W. Kimball urged us to "get a notebook, . . . a journal that will last through all time, and maybe the angels may quote from it for eternity. Begin today and write in it your goings and comings, your deepest thoughts, your achievements and your failures, your associations and your triumphs, your impressions and your testimonies." [71] Those angels he spoke of, who will repeat what we left on record, will be biased in our favor. They may even adore us because they will be of our kin and lineage.

The opening saga of the Book of Mormon tells of a band of brothers sent into mortal danger that they might claim some old family records.

Nephi found it necessary to convince two of these young men that their job was supremely important, well worth risking life and limb. After all, the records would prove precious to their children someday (1 Nephi 3:19–20).

We are not told just how Nephi's hearers, who were still not even married, felt about this gift to their unborn and unimagined children of the distant future. Such a thing would not occur to most people even if they did have children. That Nephi would think of it hints at his depth and maturity. Facing down Laban and his murderous cronies over an old book so your descendants could someday read it? In the logic of eternity, "Of course."

Nephi pointed out that these records would preserve "the language of our fathers" (1 Nephi 3:19). He was not just speaking of the Hebrew tongue or of Egyptian characters. It means a lot to hear the truth in the words of your ancestors—not only their words but also their expression of ideas, their personal appreciations. In his devotion to obtain that precious record, Nephi ensured a link between past and future. Generations past would be an inspiration to countless millions in the future.

Each of us is a link, a Joseph in Egypt, a Moroni, an Abraham, or an Adam or Eve, connecting the great past and the untold future with eternity. "We labor diligently to write," Nephi said, "to persuade our children, and also our brethren, to believe in Christ" (2 Nephi 25:23; Abraham 1:31). We write in remembrance not only of what is important but also of Who is important. After all, he who means everything to us now will mean no less to those who live centuries from now. We trust him, and we can say why. They who will trust our words will need to trust him too.

NOTES

1. Spencer W. Kimball, *The Teachings of Spencer W. Kimball*, ed. Edward L. Kimball (Salt Lake City: Bookcraft, 1982), 297.
2. The First Presidency and Council of the Twelve Apostles, "The Family—A Proclamation to the World," *Ensign*, November 1995, 102.
3. M. Russell Ballard, *Counseling with Our Councils* (Salt Lake City: Deseret Book, 1997), 151.
4. Boyd K. Packer, "'The Shield of Faith,'" *Ensign*, May 1995, 9.
5. David O. McKay, in Conference Reports of The Church of Jesus Christ of Latter-day Saints (Salt Lake City: The Church of Jesus Christ of Latter-day Saints, 1898 to present), April 1964, 5.
6. Ibid., April 1935, 116.
7. Wilford Woodruff, in *Collected Discourses*, comp. Brian H. Stuy, 5 vols. (Burbank, Calif.: B.H.S. Publishing, 1987–92), 1:326.
8. Letter from the First Presidency to all members of the Church, in Russell M. Nelson, "Set in Order Thy House," *Ensign*, November 2001, 70.
9. Stephen L Richards, in *Where Is Wisdom?* (Salt Lake City: Deseret Book, 1955), 36.
10. Letter from the First Presidency to all members of the Church, in Randal A. Wright, *Why Say No When the World Says Yes* (Salt Lake City: Deseret Book, 1993), 100–101.
11. Spencer W. Kimball, "Living the Gospel in the Home," *Ensign*, May 1978, 101.
12. Spencer W. Kimball, *The Teachings of Spencer W. Kimball*, 117.
13. Nathan Eldon Tanner, *BYU Speeches of the Year* (Provo, Utah: BYU Press, 17 May 1966), 11.
14. David O. McKay, in Conference Report, October 1969, 7.
15. Brigham Young, in *Journal of Discourses*, 26 vols. (London: Latter-day Saints' Book Depot, 1854–86), 2:90.
16. Joseph F. Smith, in *Messages of the First Presidency*, ed. James R. Clark, 6 vols. (Salt Lake City: Bookcraft, 1965–75), 5:64
17. Gordon B. Hinckley, in "Messages of Inspiration from President Hinckley," *Church News*, 2 September 1995, 2.
18. George Q. Cannon, in *Collected Discourses*, 4:304.
19. George Albert Smith, in Conference Report, April 1949, 190.
20. Ezra Taft Benson, "To the Single Adult Brethren of the Church," *Ensign*, April 1988, 53.
21. Howard W. Hunter, "Being a Righteous Husband and Father," *Ensign*, November 1994, 50.
22. Russell M. Nelson, "Personal Priesthood Responsibility," *Ensign*, November 2003, 46.

23. Howard W. Hunter, "Being a Righteous Husband and Father," 51.

24. The First Presidency, in *Messages of the First Presidency,* 6:5.

25. Gordon B. Hinckley, "Our Responsibility to Our Young Women," *Ensign,* September 1988, 11.

26. George Albert Smith, *Millennial Star,* 9 March 1933, 173.

27. Harold B. Lee, in *Teachings of Presidents of the Church: Harold B. Lee* (Salt Lake City: The Church of Jesus Christ of Latter-day Saints, 2000), 140.

28. Ezra Taft Benson, "To the Single Adult Sisters of the Church," *Ensign,* November 1988, 97.

29. Ezra Taft Benson, *Come, Listen to a Prophet's Voice* (Salt Lake City: Deseret Book, 1990), 60.

30. Brigham Young, in *Journal of Discourses,* 8:208.

31. Spencer W. Kimball, *Faith Precedes the Miracle* (Salt Lake City: Deseret Book, 1975), 132.

32. Reed Smoot, in Conference Report, April 1903, 54.

33. George Albert Smith, in Conference Report, October 1907, 38–39.

34. Russell M. Nelson, "How Firm Our Foundation," *Ensign,* May 2002, 76.

35. Reed Smoot, in Conference Report, April 1903, 54.

36. George Albert Smith, in Conference Report, October 1948, 166.

37. Gordon B. Hinckley, "Save the Children," *Ensign,* November 1994, 54.

38. Neal A. Maxwell, *That My Family Should Partake* (Salt Lake City: Deseret Book, 1974), 120–21.

39. The First Presidency, in Neal A. Maxwell, *That My Family Should Partake,* 121.

40. Brigham Young, in *Journal of Discourses,* 11:117.

41. Joseph Smith, *Teachings of the Prophet Joseph Smith,* 240.

42. Joseph F. Smith, *Gospel Doctrine* (Salt Lake City: Deseret Book, 1975), 316.

43. Boyd K. Packer, "Our Moral Environment," *Ensign,* May 1992, 68.

44. Marvin J. Ashton, "'If Thou Endure It Well,'" *Ensign,* November 1984, 21.

45. Harold B. Lee, in *Teachings of Presidents of the Church: Harold B. Lee,* 136.

46. Joseph Smith, *History of The Church of Jesus Christ of Latter-day Saints,* ed. B. H. Roberts, 2d ed. rev., 7 vols. (Salt Lake City: The Church of Jesus Christ of Latter-day Saints, 1932–51), 5:530.

47. Howard W. Hunter, "Parents' Concern for Children," *Ensign,* November 1983, 64–65.

48. Brigham Young Jr., in Conference Report, October 1898, 49.

49. Joseph Smith, in *They Knew the Prophet,* comp. Hyrum L. Andrus and Helen Mae Andrus (Salt Lake City: Bookcraft, 1974), 100.

50. Spencer W. Kimball, *The Teachings of Spencer W. Kimball,* 117.

51. Gordon B. Hinckley, "Benediction," *Ensign,* May 2003, 99.

52. Gordon B. Hinckley, *Teachings of Gordon B. Hinckley* (Salt Lake City: Deseret Book, 1997), 211.

53. Ibid., 211–12.

54. L. Tom Perry, *Living with Enthusiasm* (Salt Lake City: Deseret Book, 1996), 32.

55. Henry B. Eyring, "An Enduring Testimony of the Mission of the Prophet Joseph," *Ensign*, November 2003, 91.

56. Ezra Taft Benson, "The Power of the Word," *Ensign*, May 1986, 81.

57. Marion G. Romney, in Ezra Taft Benson, "Cleansing the Inner Vessel," *Ensign*, May 1986, 6.

58. Ezra Taft Benson, *The Teachings of Ezra Taft Benson* (Salt Lake City: Bookcraft, 1988), 517.

59. Howard W. Hunter, *The Teachings of Howard W. Hunter,* ed. Clyde J. Williams (Salt Lake City: Deseret Book, 2002), 241.

60. John A. Widstoe, "The House of the Lord," *Improvement Era,* April 1936, 228.

61. John A. Widstoe, "Gathering Genealogical Records," *Improvement Era,* January 1935, 39.

62. The First Presidency and Council of the Twelve Apostles, "The Family—A Proclamation to the World," 102.

63. Ezra Taft Benson, *The Teachings of Ezra Taft Benson,* 146–47.

64. Spencer W. Kimball, "Living the Gospel in the Home," 101.

65. J. Reuben Clark Jr., in Thomas S. Monson, "Bring Him Home," *Ensign*, November 2003, 58.

66. M. Russell Ballard, "Let Our Voices Be Heard," *Ensign*, November 2003, 16.

67. Bob Steinike, in "How to Smoothly Adjust to Marriage," *Church News,* 11 February 1995, 15.

68. Joseph Smith, *Teachings of the Prophet Joseph Smith,* 240.

69. Gordon B. Hinckley, "Each a Better Person," *Ensign*, November 2002, 100.

70. Spencer W. Kimball, *President Kimball Speaks Out* (Salt Lake City: Deseret Book, 1981), 55.

71. Spencer W. Kimball, *The Teachings of Spencer W. Kimball,* 351.

PART C
PROMISES FOR THE LATTER-DAY CHURCH

No people on the face of the globe watch the trend of world events with deeper interest than do the Latter-day Saints. Theirs is a world church, and occurrences everywhere have a broader significance to them than to most other people. —Melvin J. Ballard[1]

Every world problem may be solved by obedience to the principles of the gospel of Jesus Christ. —David O. McKay[2]

Our time will be supremely historic and our Church will be the capstone and summation of the ages. The heavens stand ready to make it so and only wait for us to put our hands and hearts to the work. Our abilities are merely human, that is true, and our callings seem modest. But turning our labors into something eternal is God's project, not ours. He specializes in such miracles. He promises them.

51.
THIS IS THE GREAT HOUR

The building up of Zion is a cause that has interested the people of God in every age; it is a theme upon which prophets, priests and kings have dwelt with peculiar delight; they have looked forward with joyful anticipation to the day in which we live; and fired with heavenly and joyful anticipations they have sung and written and prophesied of this our day . . . we are the favored people that God has made choice of to bring about the Latter-day glory.
—Joseph Smith[3]

A particular group of workers will usher in the most historic moment in history. They will be thrilled as Zion becomes a reality. They will relieve innocent people who are in great distress. Their minds will be continually expanded by holy knowledge. They will labor with the nobles of earth and heaven. The magnificent Christ will come into their presence and minister to them in love. That fortunate people will possibly accomplish more of significance and experience more fulfillment than any people who ever lived. Who are they, these historic and fortunate ones? The people of the covenant, the workers in Christ's true Church of today—you and I.

"This is the great time foreseen by prophets since the Creation," Henry B. Eyring testified. No longer is it necessary to speak of some great work just around the corner. It is here. "The last, great gathering has begun."[4] Though mankind generally hasn't noticed yet, the latter-day glory is bursting forth at this very moment. They cannot yet see that the true

Church is infinitely more than the churches of the world. They don't notice, but we must.

You and I know that the Church is the agent and host of the latter-day glory—a vast power station that houses, synchronizes, and distributes the powers of heaven on earth. As a prophet said, "This Church, I submit, is far more than a social organization. . . . It is more than sacrament meeting, more even than temple service. It is the kingdom of God on the earth."[5]

Soon enough, Christ will reveal himself and publicly own his Church. So near and real is that hour that living prophets gave this solemn assurance as the new century began: "We testify that He will someday return to earth. 'And the glory of the Lord shall be revealed, and all flesh shall see it together' (Isaiah 40:5). . . . Every knee shall bend and every tongue shall speak in worship before Him. Each of us will stand to be judged of Him."[6] Wonder of wonders, that time is ours.

But this glory cannot unfurl without us. This is no time to be distracted. The history of the world patiently awaits our hands. Spencer W. Kimball stood before the Church in 1979 and said: "This impression weighs upon me—that the Church is at a point in its growth and maturity when we are at last ready to move forward in a major way. . . . The basic decisions needed for us to move forward, as a people, must be made by the individual members of the Church. The major strides which must be made by the Church will follow upon the major strides to be made by us as individuals. We have paused on some plateaus long enough."[7]

Surely the urgency is greater now than it was in 1979.

52.
A Time for Optimism

It is a wonderful time to be a member of the Church. I envy these young people who are here today. Their lives are ahead of them. They will see marvelous things in the years that lie ahead. I have no doubt of it whatever. The Church will grow and grow and grow, and no force under the heavens can stop it.
—Gordon B. Hinckley[8]

We are always interested when an underdog team rises to the top of the league and wins the championship. The human heart responds when someone defies the odds, does the impossible, rises over ironclad ironies. We were created to love tales of heroism. There will be none greater than the story of Christ and his people doing his marvelous work. That tale already hints of unlikely and superhuman progress. But the story is just getting started. While the Church attracts the anger and slander of dark forces, it will move forward. It will become the fascination of the world.

There was once a family pet, an enormous white Labrador retriever named Tank. He was named after his size, shape, and personality. He was a dog of amazing loyalty, especially toward his master, one of the sons in the family. They were together every available hour. On one memorable occasion, the boy was in a motorboat with some friends. Tank was on the dock, his body and eyes intent on the boat as it moved across the small lake. It happened that someone with two

Doberman pinschers parked by the dock and let his dogs out for a run. These two saw Tank looking out on the water and couldn't resist the chance for some adventure. They sped down the dock ramp and raced toward the big white target in hopes of a good fight.

Tank seemed to pay no heed as the Dobermans closed in from both sides, snarling, baring their teeth, baiting and biting and diving in at will. Tank stayed on his feet somehow, his gaze still fixed on his master, whose boat was now making another pass. When the boat was out of sight, Tank suddenly turned on the attackers. What happened then was too fast to see clearly. Great muscles rippled under his heavy coat, and Tank seemed to make only two moves, the first resulting in a dark shape yelping and splashing into the water on one side of the dock. The move that came next caused the other dog to do the same thing on the other side of the dock. In the next instant, it seemed, his ears and coat a bit tattered, Tank had forgotten his assailants and was again watching for his master.

We are not frightened about the future of the Church, even when it seems to have assailants, because "no force under the heavens can stop it." As forces and opponents think to stop the work, how will we stay calm? How will we feel the assurance that the prophets feel? The answer is simple. We must keep our eyes on the Master.

Latter-day Saints are as aware as anyone that clouds are gathering. But more than any others, we are of good cheer. We trust the mighty Father and his Son. We know a blaze of light and joy is coming. We feel as our prophet does: "I feel so optimistic about this Church, so very, very optimistic. . . . It's true. Be happy about it."[9]

53.
BLESSING THE NATIONS

I am positive that the blessings of the Lord will attend every country which opens its gates to the gospel of Christ. Their blessings will flow in education, and culture, and faith, and love, like Enoch's city of Zion, which was translated, and also will become like the 200 years of peaceful habitation in this country in Nephite days. There will come prosperity to the nations, comfort and luxuries to the people, joy and peace to all recipients, and eternal life to those who accept and magnify it.

—Spencer W. Kimball [10]

Righteousness leads to great favors; those favors inspire more righteousness. This cycle repeats itself forever, revolutionizing an individual or a whole nation, provided the cycle doesn't die in apathy or pride. But where does the cycle begin? What comes first, the blessing or the goodness?

At first we might suppose that the righteousness comes first. For example, an individual must reach out for the gospel. Or in the case of a nation, leaders must accept enough light to open their borders and doors. But there is a step before that. Something must stir hope and interest, giving the individual or the group some reason to reach for the truth. Somewhere outside themselves they must perceive a treasure worth inviting in. The first move lies with us who already have the treasure. As the spark or flame that makes possible another fire, we need to have the cycle well established and open to view, ready to transfer to other lives.

Once the cycle begins, blessings mount up in every category. When God prospers people in the land, he is more generous than they could have imagined. The oldest and sweetest storyline in human history is "the blessed and happy state of those that keep the commandments of God. For behold, they are blessed in all things, both temporal and spiritual" (Mosiah 2:41).

At a critical moment in history, after the ground was softened and conditions were right, the gospel seed was planted in American soil. Some rejected it, but the plant grew because others embraced it. Suppose the gospel had been refused by everyone in America. Of course, the Church would not have been established. But that isn't all. American history, and world history for that matter, would now read differently.

What different role would war have taken? Would America have survived the Civil War? Would freedom have been preserved? Would knowledge have flourished? Would America have been prospered or swept away? (Ether 2:7–8; D&C 136:34–36).

And what of you and me? How would our histories now read if we had been less righteous? The seed must grow in us and then be planted elsewhere. The flame must be bright in us so that others will welcome it. The sweet cycle must be started in other people and other groups.

The destiny of the Church is not only to survive the world but also to revive it and to bless every honest life. "We have seen only the foreshadowing of the mighty force for good that this Church will become," said Gordon B. Hinckley.[11] The world has one hope—the Savior's saving program and priesthood. "This alone," said Brigham Young, "can deliver the human family from all the evils which now afflict its members."[12]

We are called to be a blessed people so that we can start the cycle of blessings everywhere on earth.

54.
THE PROMISE OF FREEDOM

We believe the people of the United States shall, by precept and example, bring self-government and free institutions to the peoples of the earth. We believe America will stand to all the world as the Apostle of the great doctrines. . . . When America shall fully meet this measure of conduct, it will reach its destiny in the earth. Then America will take her true place as a leader among the nations, and her principles, her ideals, her laws, shall fill the earth.
—J. Reuben Clark Jr.[13]

There came a time during the Civil War when America's survival seemed impossible. A few months for settling the conflict had turned into years of horror. Just when Union forces needed greater numbers, they were shrinking from death and desertion. But patriotism soared when Julia Ward Howe wrote "The Battle Hymn of the Republic." It reminded the soldiers that freedom is related to holiness and that both of these human privileges are worth giving up life. It went to the heart of the matter and to the hearts of young soldiers who were facing death at the cannon's mouth:

> *Christ was born across the sea,*
> *With a glory in His bosom*
> *That transfigures you and me.*
> *As he died to make men holy,*
> *Let us die to make men free.*[14]

At stake was not only the future of America but also the future of mankind. The Church cannot spread the gospel if people are not free to hear its fulness. We can't draw people into the fold of God if they aren't perfectly free to come. From the sons and daughters of liberty come sons and daughters of Christ. The promise of the Church is entwined with the promise of freedom. America's mission is essential to the mission of the Church.

"I have a feeling in my heart that the United States has a glorious destiny to fulfil," said Joseph F. Smith, "and that part of that glorious destiny is to extend liberty to the oppressed, as far as it is possible to all nations, to all people."[15]

How can the mantle of freedom spread from one single land of promise? And how can America's light shine if there is conflict and darkness in her own borders? The answer is good people and truth. Good people, if they are free and have the truth before them, do heroic things. "I believe in the soul of the American people," Anthony W. Ivins declared, "and that they will rise in their majesty when the truth becomes known."[16]

From the beginning, it was intended that God's precious gifts would "spread out from these mountain valleys into this great land of America, and from thence to the very remote corners of the earth, in order that people may be given the opportunity of embracing the gospel of Christ, which is the true law of liberty."[17]

As when America was saved during the Civil War, good people will fill America's mission to the nations.

55.

PEOPLE WILL APPROVE WHEN THEY SEE

I feel it is only a question of time, if we do our part, until most of our Father's children who are in the world and do not now understand, will learn of the truth and will be glad to be identified with the Church of Jesus Christ of Latter-day Saints.

—George Albert Smith[18]

Evidently, all people now on earth once loved the gospel, voted for it, fought for it, and perhaps taught it. The gospel truth we teach to mankind is mankind's very own ancient religion. Unfortunately, mankind has amnesia. Of course, we teach anyway—amid all the forgetfulness.

It would be nice if the teaching atmosphere in this world resembled the premortal one. Surrounding information would fit with the sacred center, the soul of each listener would be focused and peaceful. But an ideal mortal classroom is another rare luxury. Satan knows our message is coming, and he plants weeds where we would sow truth. He raises distractions. He hires hecklers. He circulates lies and groundless complaints to the unschooled. He is the prince of the world in which we teach (John 12:31; 14:30).

On the other hand, he is not the king. Satan's brash and brazen battle is doomed. Nothing can prevent the restored gospel from being widely embraced, for it is timeless and precious and true. This triumph will come both in the field of religion and in the realm of science. Adam S. Bennion assured us that "one day there will be brought together in complete harmony the full findings of truth in science and the full findings of truth as revealed by God."[19] Each truth will be a firm ally to other truths.

The secular world may not intend to support the kingdom of God, but it does anyway. How could we reach all nations, how could we notice and nourish each individual on our worldwide rolls if we were still getting around on horseback and keeping track of everything with a bottle of ink and a quill pen? And yet the Governor of the universe has only just started sharing his secrets with scientists and engineers. Greater tools will increase our reach as we need them.

The tools of man will play into the Lord's hands, but the Lord's own special tools may surprise us even more. For example, consider these declarations from Bruce R. McConkie regarding the Book of Mormon:

- "Few men on earth, either in or out of the Church, have caught the vision of what the Book of Mormon is all about."[20]
- "The Book of Mormon shall so affect men that the whole earth and all its peoples will have been influenced and governed by it."[21]
- "There is no greater issue ever to confront mankind in modern times than this: Is the Book of Mormon the mind and will and voice of God to all men?"[22]

The "wonder," the "strange act" our Father has in mind will be just that—to all of us (Isaiah 29:14; D&C 101:95). In this time of serious work, the marvelous part has only begun.

56.
HE NEVER FAILS HIS CHURCH

No cause under heaven can stop the work of God. Adversity may raise its ugly head. The world may be troubled with wars and rumors of wars, but this cause will go forward.
—Gordon B. Hinckley[23]

Todd was pretty normal in childhood. Then in adolescence came his unusual craving to be outdoors. When he wasn't out exploring or camping or fishing, he was doing these things in his daydreams. His parents worried that Todd's life was out of balance. But a change was in store for him. It would be a transformation from the wholesome to the holy, from good to great.

As he cooperated with Church assignments and meetings, he was tempered. He began to read the scriptures each day, and this enlarged his heart. Finally the unselfish life of a missionary revealed to him that there were more beautiful things on the earth than the earth itself. Todd's parents saw this and said to themselves, "Our son is growing up."

When he married Kimberly, another world opened up. Here was one on whom he could focus his love without reservation, in whose service he could use all of his abilities as a protector and provider and companion. The natural world still had a place in his heart, but it could not compete with his interest in this one person, his wife.

Jesus spoke of the kind of love that causes us to make our life into a gift for someone else as the *greatest* love (John 15:13). That kind of love is advanced maturity and leads us in the path of joy. It is with the grownup and protective love of a perfect husband that the Lord devotes himself to his Church. Because of this love, he will never fail or abandon us, his people.

Isaiah said to Israel, "Thy Maker is thine husband" (Isaiah 54:5; Jeremiah 3:20). In the New Testament, the bride is not Israel in general but specifically the Church (Ephesians 5:23; Revelation 21:2). Jehovah's devotion is not like that of an average husband or even of an unusually nice husband, but rather of a perfect husband. The marriage-like relationship between the Lord and his people is similar to *his* kind of marriage—celestial marriage.

The Lord doesn't oversee the Church with mild interest. His watching is careful every moment. History shows that his devotion is perfect and unswerving. Spencer W. Kimball asked, "Can you find in all the holy scriptures where the Lord Jesus Christ ever failed his church?"[24]

Some of Enoch's people could have felt doomed and outnumbered as the rest of the world bore down on them (Moses 7:13, 17–23). Perhaps the eight passengers on the ark wondered if they had been forgotten as their long vigil on the waters swayed on (Genesis 7:7–24). Members of Alma's little congregation, secluded in a vast mountain wilderness, may have felt alone and very small (Mosiah 18:34–35; 23:1–5, 21–24). But never did the God of heaven take his eyes from these people. His saw them through it all. Their stories prove what our stories will someday prove—his support for his beloved Church is all-powerful, his love unsleeping.

57.
TRIUMPH IS
SURE

The Standard of Truth has been erected; no unhallowed hand can stop the work from progressing; persecutions may rage, mobs may combine, armies may assemble, calumny may defame, but the truth of God will go forth boldly, nobly, and independent, till it has penetrated every continent, visited every clime, swept every country, and sounded in every ear, till the purposes of God shall be accomplished, and the Great Jehovah shall say the work is done.

—Joseph Smith[25]

In former days, there would come a breathless moment on the field of battle when the flag of some mighty force was raised. Satan faced such a moment, agonizing in his angry heart, when he beheld the banner of God's restored Church rising over the fray, marking a new dispensation. The armies of light were taking the field. The tide of history would change. The gates of salvation would slowly swing open to waiting millions. The raising of that flag or "standard" marks not the finish but the start of the work. Once begun, it could not be stopped.

Satan does what he can and with inhuman frenzy. He cannot see that his cause is futile, for he has gone mad. An enemy this furious and irrational can take many out with him. We do not face him casually. Nevertheless, we go at our tasks in the Church without fear, "boldly, nobly, and independent." When his calumny—his sneering accusation—comes our way, we try not to take it personally, for it is really aimed at our Master (Matthew 24:9; 1 Nephi

11:33–35). We are honored, in fact, to be disliked by those who so dislike him (Matthew 5:11–12).

Of course, we cannot take God's triumph too personally either. It is not our triumph and not our truth. The purposes of God, not our purposes, will be accomplished. The work of Jehovah, not our work, will be done when he says it is done. So we do not worry very much about public opinion. Public opinion never did know much about the missing people of Enoch. Public opinion had long been drowned out before Noah's family started their new world. Public opinion never did learn the wonderful mercies poured out on Alma's little ward in the wilderness when at last it merged with the main body of the Saints in Zarahemla.

The reason for the triumph is not to prove to snickering bad guys that they were profoundly mistaken about us. We will not be shoving the light into their faces. We won't be gaggling out the back window, "We told you so." We will set things right ever so patiently. Our motive is to bless those who despitefully use us and persecute us (Matthew 5:44). That is, we want to reclaim as many bad guys as possible, so we pray for the softening of their hearts and the opening of their eyes. This will take time. We will move slowly and kindly, neither in fear nor in haste. If we saw through their eyes, perhaps we would need someone to be patient with us.

We insult or distrust our God when we wonder if his work will triumph at last. "There is never reason to despair," Gordon B. Hinckley proclaimed. "This is the work of God. Notwithstanding the efforts of all who oppose it, it will go forward as the God of heaven has designed it should do."[26]

The God of heaven has designed his Church and his work to triumph.

131

58.
EVIL WILL FALL

In the midst of all the troubles, the uncertainties, the tumult and chaos through which the world is passing, almost unnoticed by the majority of the people of the world, there has been set up a kingdom, a kingdom over which God the Father presides, and Jesus the Christ is the King. That kingdom is rolling forward, as I say, partly unnoticed, but it is rolling forward with a power and a force that will stop the enemy in its tracks while some of you live.

—Hugh B. Brown[27]

The enemy, who has hounded good people from before the creation of the earth, is on a track. Satan has a purpose, a goal, a plan. He intends to defeat our Father, topple his kingdom, and steal his children. But Satan will be foiled again and again, and he and his hosts will be soundly defeated, altogether stopped in their tracks. The Father's power, vested in his Son and rolling forth in his work, will always prove vastly superior to Satan's.

Joseph Smith taught a basic principle: "The closer we observe the celestial law, the more opposition we shall meet."[28] It stands to reason that the more faithful we are, the more desperate the enemy will be, and therefore the more stern will be our battle.

That principle is visible in story after story of God's work in every stage of history. Like a negative mirror, the people of Noah's time reflected the righteousness of Noah's family among terrible and widespread wickedness (Moses 8:13, 16, 18, 22). As the people of Enoch grew more righteous, their opponents became more bitter and violent (Moses 7:13–17, 68–69). As Alma's fellow disciples lived the gospel more perfectly in their wilderness refuge, they found themselves surrounded by ruthless enemies (Mosiah 24:7–11).

But there is another principle, also proven by the history of faithful people: Though the powers of evil are horrified by righteousness, and though they oppose it in every way, righteous people are never safer and never more secure in the arms of their Savior than when they are living his gospel. Those whom Satan would most like to defeat are the very ones most sheltered from his attack.

Stories of the past tell us much about the future. Of course we will see a rising opposition to the work of the Lord. But that opposition, so intimidating to the natural man, will never amount to much compared to the might and power of Christ.

In the premortal life, when the time finally came for Satan to be removed, he was "cast down" by the power of Christ (Moses 4:3). Jesus routinely controlled evil spirits during his mortal ministry. Then, in Gethsemane and on the cross, his victory over evil was complete. Thanks to that special victory, all of his future victories are certain. As Richard G. Scott testified, "Because of the Atonement of the Savior, the plan of happiness will succeed and Satan's plan is doomed to failure."[29]

When the time comes for evil to fall in the latter days, to be cast down again, it will fall completely (Revelation 18:2–23). To Christ's people on earth, it will come as a relief but not as a surprise.

59.
HAPPINESS IN THE LAST DAYS

As the tapestry of [Church history] has unrolled, a beautiful pattern has come to view. It finds expression in the lives of a happy and wonderful people. It portends marvelous things yet to come.

—Gordon B. Hinckley[30]

The "beautiful pattern"—the pattern of happiness—is already noticeable to some. It will be more obvious as time passes. We have only begun to see the beauty of that pattern. We have only begun to see the glory of Church history. We have only begun to see for ourselves how happy a people can be.

If we leave out the latter-day promise of happiness, we will misunderstand the latter days. To think of dark clouds only—with no linings of shimmering silver, no golden shafts bursting through, no sheltered and shining Zion on earth, and no great people singing songs of joy among the nations—is to conjure up a naive and distorted picture. It ignores too many prophecies (Isaiah 35:10; D&C 45:67–71; 101:18–19; 133:29–34). A "happy and wonderful people" is one of the signs that God is at work among his children.

Enoch lived near sorrow as we do, and yet the Lord said to him, "Thou shalt abide in me, and I in you; therefore walk with me" (Moses 6:34). His people were opposed on all sides as we could be, and yet "the Lord blessed the land, and they were blessed . . . and did flourish" (Moses 7:17). Enoch's people knew a world torn apart by criticism and countercriticism, a world something like the one we know today. And yet, "they were of one heart and one mind, and dwelt in righteousness" (Moses 7:18).

Enoch saw *us* and our world. He saw our time in history, a time that "great tribulations shall be among the children of men." Then the Lord uttered to Enoch, and to us, this grand reassurance: "But my people will I preserve" (Moses 7:61, 67). Whenever we see storms coming our way, we can remember that promise.

Along with that preserving we can expect happiness (Psalms 144:15; 146:5). It is not a mere decoration that can fall off the tree of a righteous person's life. It is a part of that life, a sure fruit growing out of the tree (Galatians 5:22–23). It comes because, as Nephi said, we live "after the manner of happiness" (2 Nephi 5:27; James 5:11; 1 Peter 3:14; 4:14.) If we live after that pattern, it is wired right into our soul.

No evil day or evil person can burglarize something so private as happiness any more than the Grinch could steal Christmas. Satan "must operate within bounds set by the Lord," said Richard G. Scott. "He cannot take away any blessing that has been earned. He cannot alter character that has been woven from righteous decisions."[31]

So the promise of happiness applies to our good times and our tough times, to momentous times and to small moments. "However dark conditions may seem in this world today," said Robert D. Hales, "whatever the storms we are facing personally, in our homes and in our families, this joy can be ours now."[32] That faithful people will be even happier in the days ahead is just one of the "marvelous things yet to come."

60.
A DRAMATIC
WORK

We are engaged in a great eternal struggle that concerns the very souls of the sons and daughters of God. We are not losing. We are winning. We will continue to win if we will be faithful and true.
—Gordon B. Hinckley[33]

The evening before they were to purchase a new motor home, Roger and Betty were asked to work with the young single adults in their stake. The stake president held up a file folder full of lists and said with concern, "There are over 200 names there, all of them between 18 and 30, but there may be more." He glanced through the pages as he had so often before and set it down on the desk in front of the couple.

"Some of those people are college graduates; some never finished high school. Some are returned missionaries; others haven't been in a Church meeting for years. All of them need each other socially and spiritually," the president said. "Please find them and work with them and get them together. Consider them your grandchildren."

On their way home, Roger drove while Betty carefully read all the names aloud, one by one. "Well," she said softly, "what do you think?"

"I'm thinking we've got way too many grandchildren to be driving around in a motor home."

We come to mortal life to finish building our souls, the last and toughest part of a long project. It is a battle, and no one can win it alone. Others help us; we help others. Oddly, the battle for souls is enjoyable and, by and large, is a satisfying partnership between friends. We don't nag or force or argue in the Lord's work. We don't save souls by being stiff or reluctant or worn out. The yoke we wear in the army of Christ, according to his own description, is "easy" (Matthew 11:30).

What is the cost of victory? Everything, in a way. But since "everything" belongs to the Creator, it costs nothing of our own. Nothing except our hearts, our plans, our loyalty. In other words, the work of saving souls is a work of love. And that means we can hardly call it work at all.

It was in love that God inspired the stake president to meet with Roger and Betty. Not often does anyone buy a motor home out of real love, but love did prompt this couple to accept their call and go to work. It was in love that a few young adults, and then a few more, attended the stake institute class and other activities organized by Roger and Betty.

The resulting friendships and spiritual experiences, the activated lives and testimonies, and the mission calls and temple marriages were typical fruits of the great battle for souls. Love makes the struggle seem easy. Love makes the cost of time seem like no cost at all.

Time is our major offering in this battle. Souls are saved slowly. We give some of that time in private—preparing a lesson, organizing a service project, hunting for an address, preparing a name for temple work. Or we may spend it in small favors that slowly build a friendship. But *time,* what is that? We are doing something that lasts forever. With our gift of time, we are finishing the project and fighting the war of the ages. With love and time, we win eternity.

61.

SPECIAL WORKERS ARE ON THE WAY

The Lord has chosen a small number of choice spirits of sons and daughters out of all the creations of God, who are to inherit this earth; and this company of choice spirits have been kept in the spirit world for six thousand years to come forth in the last days to stand in the flesh in this last dispensation of the fulness of times, to organize the kingdom of God upon the earth, to build it up and to defend it.

—Wilford Woodruff[34]

Out of moving experience, Moses once said, "The Lord is a man of war" (Exodus 15:3). Bullies and odds are never an issue with him. He makes his moves with perfect timing and wins when he prefers to win. He lets each wave of troops give its all on the field before sending others. He allows us to strain and grow before we win the crown. He has special warriors in reserve for special times. At our pivotal moment in history, he is sending selected spirits suited for this time.

There was such a time in Nephite history (Alma 56:38–51). The small army of Antipus had been gaining on an army of Lamanites, which outnumbered them. Antipus's goal was to prevent the Lamanites from attacking Helaman's youthful force, who were being used as decoys.

But now the enemy, after a night of sleep, suddenly turned about to give merciless battle to the men of Antipus, who had been rushing at double speed all night to reach them. The weary Nephite soldiers were nearly overrun as the Lamanites sent one fresh group after another upon them. Who came to the rescue? Those "very young" boys chose to be more than decoys after all (Alma 56:46). They turned back and fought murderous men bigger and older and harder than they.

The veteran Antipus died in that battle. But before he closed his eyes he may have seen those young men charging across the landscape. Perhaps the last thoughts in that heroic heart of his were sweetened because these young warriors "fought as if with the strength of God; yea, never were men known to have fought with such miraculous strength" (Alma 56:56).

In our own crucial battle, older soldiers are trying stoutly to defend righteous principles and sacred ground. The opposition is more numerous and angry than we expected. A wave of giants will arrive just as the world most needs their fresh example, their unique leadership, and their kind ministering. Where are those giants now?

Ezra Taft Benson answered, "In the veins of these boys and girls in your Primary organizations flows some of the best blood that this world has ever known."[35] By no accident, the most nourishing book ever published is going to every nation, with all sorts of study helps, just as this multitude of giants enters our homes and classrooms. President Benson pointed out that the Book of Mormon is perfectly suited "to rear a generation that can redeem Zion."[36]

Speaking to some of these young giants, Boyd K. Packer said, "I think of the joy and happiness that await you in this life and the work you are to do, and I cannot be discouraged."[37] Though everything is at stake, everything has been arranged by the Man of War. Reinforcements are on the way.

62.

WORK WILL BLESS US FOREVER

Nothing happens in this Church unless you work. It is like a wheelbarrow. It doesn't move until you get ahold of the two handles and push. Hard work moves the work of the Lord forward, and if you have learned to work with real integrity it will bless your lives forever. I mean that with all my heart. It will bless your lives forever.

—Gordon B. Hinckley[38]

Elder Carter awoke and saw through his little window the familiar sight of Pusan's upper city, shining pink in the dawn. It was 5:30 A.M., and the sounds of a workday were already stirring. *Work.* That was one of the things President Hinckley had mentioned at their combined missionary meeting a couple of days before. The quote was on a little card next to his cot. Elder Carter picked it up and whispered the words:

"You may not bring very many converts into the Church during your mission. I do not care about that so long as you try, so long as you work hard. If you will work hard the matter of converts will take care of itself, I am satisfied of that. Give it your very best."[39]

The elder fumbled under the cot for his wallet and pulled out another quote, this one folded and worn from years of review. Again he read softly:

"To my grandson, Casey, on his tenth birthday:

"Before you get too old, I want to give you a little advice. A lot of people wouldn't say it's such a big deal, but believe me, it is. I'm talking about learning to work, just plain old doing a job.

"A lot of people know how to do a job, but I don't mean that. I mean learn to work. There's a part inside each person that doesn't especially like to do the same thing over and over or that gets bothered if a job takes too long, in their opinion. But another part of you is strong and can stay with anything that needs doing. There are a lot of people in this world that don't give that strong part a chance to develop. It seems like the weak part is always in charge. You'll run into these folks every now and then. Like some guy that gets about four minutes into a job and then you look and he's sitting down or gone to get a drink of water. He's probably a good kid, but he hasn't learned to put that strong part in charge when he's got work to do. It takes practice, Casey.

"When you have a little job to do, get at it soon. Most of the stress people talk about comes from putting things off. And once you start, stay with it, finish it, and clean up after yourself. You will feel good, I promise. You'll respect yourself, and others will notice and respect you too. I'm telling you, Casey, if you practice, you'll get to where that strong part won't back down on anything.

"And that isn't all. The Lord has special plans for people who can work. Being trusted by the Lord is about as wonderful as any feeling there is. So start now, Casey, putting that strong part of you in charge when you have a job to do, and it will just keep getting stronger. —Grandpa"

The principle is true for missionaries as well as prophets, for parents as well as children. It is true for every soul. When God gives a tool or power or advantage, it is accompanied by one simple instruction, as if stamped on the back: "Go to work." We will know the approval of the Giver when we follow that instruction.

63.
Loved As
a Friend

I promise you that if you'll use your gifts to serve someone else, you'll feel the Lord's love for that person. You'll also feel his love for you. And you'll be preparing for times when you will be called to serve people and to love them.

—Henry B. Eyring[40]

No one finds happiness by simply going out to get it. Happiness finds us. It comes indirectly as the quiet result of seeking the happiness of others. Jesus taught that law and lived it in every act. But he also infused his Church with it. In his kingdom, his friends serve and serve and serve as he would. Many are the blessings, all of them associated with joy.

The more genuine our service, the more full our joy. That was the testimony of George Albert Smith, who was famous for his kindly life: "Your happiness will be in proportion to your charity and to your kindness and to your love of those with whom you associate here on earth," he taught.[41] The Church nudges us toward happiness through calls to serve. One is in proportion to the other.

The Church could not exist more than an hour, either here or in heaven, without the unselfish work people do in their callings. Just as "God is love," his Church is a channel for his love (1 John 4:8, 16) and a network of joy (Helaman 6:3).

Carolyn was called to be president

of a struggling Young Women program in her ward. She cried and not especially with joy. She liked teenage girls, as long as she didn't have to understand them or lead them. "Teenagers scare me," she said frankly as she looked out at the girls during their first time together. The girls laughed, which didn't comfort her in the slightest. Conveniently, only seven girls attended that evening out of the twenty-nine that should have been there.

"I liked how small it was," she later said. "I was tempted to make sure no more became active. But that wasn't what the Lord had in mind when he called me. So we kept inviting and creating a good program every week as if they would all come. In a year, nearly everyone was coming, nearly every week." Now she does shed tears of joy when she speaks of her calling.

If some don't enjoy serving, it may be, as Henry B. Eyring suggested, that "they have focused on the mechanics and not the glorious opportunity."[42] Mechanics—things and timing—support what we do. But what we do is something else: We announce the good tidings of our Friend.

Gordon B. Hinckley testified of the "sweet peace in your heart that you have served your Lord. . . . You will come to know your Redeemer as your greatest friend in time or eternity."[43] This promise—that we will enjoy the love of God in his service—applies to all of us. Joseph Smith used the example of a priest in the Aaronic Priesthood, whose "enjoyment is as great as if he were one of the Presidency," if he magnifies his calling.[44]

By giving our all as the prophets do, their Master becomes our Master—a Master who doesn't just reward faithful helpers as servants but also loves them as friends (John 15:15; D&C 93:45, 51).

64.
HE WILL
MAGNIFY
YOU

*You . . . will come against the
wall. It seems to be across your
path. . . . You can walk from
here to that wall, having faith
that God will give you a ladder,
or show you a hidden ladder or
an opening, and he will do it, if
you will walk just as far as you
can in the performance of your
duty. No matter what it is or
how difficult your duty, do it;
walk that distance, and then say
in all sincerity and faith,
"Father, help me. Open up the
way for me. Give me strength to
do my duty, give me strength to
overcome temptation."*
—David O. McKay[45]

Walls—the imposing challenges and obstacles we face—have a way of making us bigger and wiser. If we had some precise way of measuring at birth and later at death the depth of a person's character, wisdom, and sensitivity of soul, we likely would find a wonderful change. The mortal journey works like magic. What is true of the journey can be true also of each wall we face along the way. If we go as far as we can and then let our Father help us, he will either open the way or make us strong.

These magnifying miracles happen all the time to those who magnify their callings in the Church. Callings have built-in walls, designed to build us. The bishop who is released is not the same as the one we sustained five years before. He is not just five years older; he is *more than* five years older. During the two thousand or so hours he spent in the bishop's office (not beating on the walls but overcoming them!) and during the twenty-four hours a day he spent holding the holy office of bishop, he may have changed more than he changed anyone else.

His family, his employer, and even his dog perhaps may have all noticed the transformation. Like a life well lived, the calling magnified *him*.

It isn't just the office of bishop. Most any calling, if we give it our best, can shake us awake to realities we had not noticed before, can invite us to be more holy, can soften us toward others, and can induce us to kneel more often before our God. This is part of being magnified.

From our Church callings and Church relationships, we learn how to fill the most important callings and how to value and nurture the most important relationships—those found in the home. For example, it isn't even necessary to be the bishop in order to learn how to interview your own child at home. We simply go to the bishop for an interview and then return home and apply what we learned.

"Even the smallest act to build faith in another person or in a family," Henry B. Eyring pointed out, "qualifies us for the gift and power of the Holy Ghost."[46] That is a key—the Holy Ghost is not necessarily drawn to those who are faithfully busy but to those who build faith in others. And once the Holy Ghost is with us, he prefers to stay with us.

Nor does diligence mean to wear ourselves down with worry. "Don't fret or get a hurrying spirit," counseled Brigham Young, a man who faced many walls.[47] Stress and fear may only mean that faith has somehow slipped—that we have somehow forgotten that God, the builder, does not fail.

65.
FOLLOW THE SPIRIT

The language of the Spirit comes to him who seeks with all his heart to know God and keep His divine commandments. Proficiency in this "language" permits one to breach barriers, overcome obstacles, and touch the human heart.

—Thomas S. Monson[48]

The Holy Ghost seeks companions to follow him, to join him in his mission. We attract the Comforter to us when we are committed to do what he does—testify, encourage, and edify. Henry B. Eyring assures us that "when we comfort others, out of our faith in the Lord, He sends the Comforter to us."[49] The power of the Holy Ghost directs his junior companions.

Of course, what we are is always a part of our message. As we serve in the Church, we radiate ourselves. "To exist," said David O. McKay, "is to be the radiation of our feelings, natures, doubts, schemes. . . . You cannot escape it. Man cannot escape for one moment the radiation of his character."[50]

Virginia is an example of radiance. She is in her nineties and doesn't often feel well. She isn't a prominent leader in her ward. But she visits often with her family and neighbors, and she meets faithfully with ward members. She is uplifting and full of faith. Recently, after personal revelation had been discussed in a Church class, she asked the teacher, "Guess what revelation I get most often?"

A little surprised, the teacher looked into her eyes and realized she was being serious. The teacher knew that Virginia read the scriptures often and wondered if she might be referring to gospel insights. Or maybe she could be getting some advanced previews about the next life. She waited for his answer. "Well, Virginia, I don't know . . ."

With a twinkle in her eye, she leaned forward and spoke in a quiet voice, as if sharing a secret: "Be of good cheer." She smiled while the teacher took that in. "That's the revelation. It comes quite often these days. 'Be of good cheer.' That's what the Lord wants me to do."

Virginia's good cheer is an act of faith. If we know that the Lord will see things through to a good result, our faith radiates with power. Our faith keeps us tireless and warm and entitles us to inspiration. The best hope for any struggling person near us is an encouraging sunshine that comes from a dependable, believing friend (1 Nephi 16:5).

The servant of the Lord, like the Lord himself, acts confidently, quickly, and often. "Our opportunities to give of ourselves are indeed limitless, but they are also perishable," Thomas S. Monson said. "There are hearts to gladden. There are kind words to say. There are gifts to be given. There are deeds to be done."[51] The urgings of the Spirit—whether to bestow words or cheer or some generous favor—are always urgent urgings. The way to detect a prompting is by its good spirit. The way to follow it is *promptly*.

"Don't postpone a prompting," President Monson counseled. Then he promised: "Rather, act on it, and the Lord will open the way."[52]

66.
KIND INFLUENCE

Assignments always should be given with the greatest love, consideration, and kindness. . . . A leader . . . must show a genuine concern and love for those under his stewardship. With faith in the Lord and humility, a priesthood leader may confidently expect divine assistance in his problems. It may require struggling and pondering, but the reward is sure.

—James E. Faust[53]

John Young raised several remarkable children—Brigham Young, for example—and was himself a beloved leader. Here is some advice he gave to other parents and leaders: "If you undertake to drive people into heaven, you will have a job on hand. . . . If we cannot lead them there, we cannot get them there at all; and if we should happen to drive a few through the gate, we should have to stand there with clubs in order to keep them there; for I can assure you that heaven is no place for any one who has to be driven in order to get him there."[54]

From this caution, we get some idea of what doesn't work, as if somewhere in our hearts we didn't already know. Tight fists and tight reins don't raise up mighty children.

It doesn't work to skip over the birthright each person has to privately decide to do what is right. To replace the conscience of another soul with your own strong will invites either weakness or rebellion. To the short-sighted, pressure seems to work. It puffs things up, giving the appearance of a big harvest, like apples filled with air.

"In the work of the Lord," Gordon B. Hinckley reminded us, "there is a more appropriate motivation than pressure." In guiding God's children, we are not authorized to use any approach but his: conversion. "When there throbs in the heart of an individual Latter-day Saint, a great and vital testimony of the truth of this work, he will be found doing his duty. . . . It is conversion that makes the difference."[55] Faith isn't built by a heavy or forceful hand.

The ancient law is that "faith cometh by hearing" (Romans 10:17; Mosiah 18:7). The people of King Benjamin, for example, will be blessed forever because of the faith they gained by trusting every word of their king's last testimony to them. We have no reason to think they would have believed his words if he had not been such a respectful leader over the years (Mosiah 2:12–16, 30–31; 5:2.) He was a witness they could love and believe. Gentleness was a key to his power.

"There are many in this audience," David O. McKay once suggested, "who can look back with gratitude to the visit of some kind man. . . . Some word of commendation, some gentle hand. . . . Personal influence—we must not lose sight of it."[56]

For faithful and respectful leaders, "the reward is sure," as James E. Faust promised. It is the reward of personally and kindly influencing the destiny of some of our Father's children.

67.
THE MIND OF
A SERVANT

We must think nobler thoughts.
We must not encourage vile
thoughts or low aspirations. We
shall radiate them if we do. If
we think noble thoughts; if we
encourage and cherish noble
aspirations, there will be that
radiation when we meet people,
especially when we associate
with them.

—David O. McKay[57]

In the ancient tradition of servants—not slaves, but highly skilled, carefully selected, well-paid, devoted helpers—the mind of the servant is focused and single while on the job. There is no intention but to serve, to enthusiastically bring to pass the hopes and designs of the master. Even if we would not like such a profession, it is our privilege to serve a perfect Master.

We can't read the minds of true servants of the Lord, but we don't need to. We sense the quality of their desires, private attitudes, mental images, and thoughts. We sometimes notice the lift that comes when someone of real nobility connects with us. A noble center, a lofty mind, cannot be pretended. Thoughts are chosen (or avoided) privately and by earnest effort.

No wonder the Lord appreciates the purity and honesty of what transpires inside of us (Psalm 24:4; Matthew 5:8; Luke 8:15; Jacob 3:1; 2 Nephi 9:14). No wonder Zion, the perfect culture, signifies the "pure in heart" (D&C 97:16, 21). The lofty path of thought is not traveled automatically and perhaps not by many.

But the gospel invites us to that path and nothing lower. The mind that steps forward—the obedient mind of a servant—beckons all of us upward.

True servants of the Lord do not seek power for the sake of power (D&C 50:26–28). They are alert for every chance to spread the benefits of their Master's atoning offering. The servant doesn't want to be the only one receiving blessings. Power is but the means of fixing and upgrading—bringing earthly matters into line with the will of the Father. That modest view of power doesn't match the worldly attitude that views position as a vertical up or down matter. "There is no up or down in Church positions," said Dallin H. Oaks. "We just move around."[58]

Many an athlete or musician or surgeon can tell us that the mind has to be specially focused. Some jobs demand a special frame of mind. Such is the work of the Lord—a work that requires the thoughts and interests of a God to freely course through the minds of the workers.

Nothing serves this purpose so perfectly as the writings of the prophets—true servants sharing noble thoughts with other true servants. Immersed in the annals and literature of the sacred, we are taught by experts. We taste the nature and worth of their work, which becomes ours. We face the enemy they faced. We drink from the same sweet spring, knowing the same truths. They hand us the torch of the same Master.

Ezra Taft Benson gave this advice from his own long experience: "I urge you to recommit yourselves to a study of the scriptures. Immerse yourselves in them daily so you will have the power of the Spirit to attend you in your callings."[59]

True servants radiate what they love and think about, what burns at the center.

68.
TEACHING PURELY AND CLEARLY

Say what God says, and say no more. Never deviate one fraction from what God tells you. . . . Give out the simple principles. A man never fails who only says what he knows. . . . Preach the first principles of the Gospel—preach them over again: you will find that day after day new ideas and additional light concerning them will be revealed to you. You can enlarge upon them so as to comprehend them clearly. You will then be able to make them more plainly understood.

—Hyrum Smith[60]

The more we study the gospel core—using the revelations to fathom its first principles—the more certain and beautiful it all becomes, and the more simply we can speak of it to others. Some gospel teachers have not yet discovered this. While preparing to teach, they may not set aside enough hours to immerse themselves in their subject. Even the simplest principles need exploration, a personal and time-consuming quest.

The prayer of a teacher may span a remarkable range. The teacher prays for guidance in lengthy preparations and in the brief teaching time, for heart to love each student, and for enough light to say what the students need. The teacher prays often for the student. Henry B. Eyring counseled teachers: "Alone, as you kneel in prayer, in great faith, express the confidence you have in them and the love you have for them."[61] In class, the student senses the friendship of the teacher but may never know that this same teacher is an advocate in private prayer before God.

Jesus compared the teacher's

influence to the yeast that spreads through a mass of bread dough. It may be as "the leaven of the Pharisees," full of toxins, or it may be pure and nourishing (Matthew 16:6; 13:33). In either case, the leaven of teaching seems to have a life of its own soon after it is received into human hearts. It pervades, changes, and enlarges, for good or ill.

"The matter of teaching is one of the greatest importance," declared Joseph Fielding Smith. "We cannot estimate its value when it is properly done; neither do we know the extent of the evil that may result if it is improperly done."[62] The enormous influence of teachers will not go unnoticed in the day of their judgment (Luke 17:1–2).

For that influence to be just right—to "give out the simple principles" and to be "more plainly understood," as Hyrum Smith said—the teacher will need, in addition to prayer, a pure heart and a mind always growing in gospel treasure (D&C 84:85; 121:35). There is nothing in the world quite like having purity and clarity, and there is no way to seem to have them if we do not. It is more crucial to prepare a teacher than to prepare a lesson.

If we are properly prepared, the Spirit will be with us in the classroom—automatic and authentic. Howard W. Hunter advised gospel teachers to "listen for the truth, hearken to the doctrine, and let the manifestation of the Spirit come as it may." Then he promised, "Stay with solid principles; teach from a pure heart. Then the Spirit will penetrate your mind and heart and every mind and heart of your students."[63]

69.
THE MIGHT OF UNITY

When you are united, your power is limitless. You can accomplish anything you wish to accomplish.
—Gordon B. Hinckley[64]

Whether we are able to do some good thing in our Father's cause depends not so much upon whether it is needed—even badly needed—but rather on our worthiness as a group, whether we have the harmony that heaven requires. How often have groups fallen short, not because of a faulty aim but because of a fault line in feelings and faith?

In the early days of the Restoration, David Whitmer tells us that Joseph "could not translate unless he was humble and possessed the right feelings towards everyone. . . . One morning when he was getting ready to continue the translation, something went wrong about the house and he was put out about it. Something that Emma, his wife, had done. Oliver and I went upstairs and Joseph came up soon after to continue the translation but he could not do anything. He could not translate a single syllable. He went downstairs, out into the orchard, and made supplication to the Lord; was gone about an hour— came back to the house, and asked Emma's forgiveness and then came upstairs where we were and then the translation went on all right."[65]

This principle relates often to our Church assignments and perhaps more often to our callings in the home. For the sake of union, it is usually best not to push people to ideas or standards that are currently out of reach. Sometimes leadership means a kind timing, sensing readiness in those we serve.

"Better to give the people something they will obey," George Q. Cannon suggested, ". . . until their capacity is enlarged and they are prepared to receive higher principles and truths. That is the way God has done with His people."[66]

It may even be that the leader himself is not so ready as he thinks he is for the next step. In any case, his job is often to pace the work so that all can walk together. If we must wait another season for that long-awaited step, let us wait in the fellowship and power of unity.

Carlos and Evania started married life in a small apartment on a small budget. Without a TV, they soon developed the habit of reading together, a tradition that continued even while they raised their children.

"In all, we have read many thousands of pages—from Church publications to adventure novels," Evania says. And what was the most important of their reading? "What the Church leaders say! I'll tell you why. One day my visiting teacher brought over a box full of old Church magazines. So each night we would read at least one of their talks or articles. We really came to know their teachings, on all sorts of subjects." Carlos added, "It's hard for us to disagree on things. Something comes up, and usually we sense what's right because we know what the Lord thinks about it."

United with each other and with our God, we have power to do all he asks (3 Nephi 26:19–20).

70.

A MIGHTY HAND IS ALWAYS GUIDING THE CHURCH

The hand of the Lord may not be visible to all. There may be many who cannot discern the workings of God's will in the progress and development of this great latter-day work, but there are those who see in every hour and in every moment of the existence of the Church, from its beginning until now, the overruling, almighty hand of him who sent his Only Begotten Son to the world to become a sacrifice for the sins of the world.
—Joseph F. Smith[67]

J oseph F. Smith bore his testimony of the Lord's guidance at a general conference in 1904. A century later, it is still so. The very work of God's kingdom, ignored or even belittled when there are not eyes to see, still lives. The miracle persists "in every hour and in every moment." President Smith pointed to the "overruling, almighty hand" that supported the earthly life of the great Messiah. That hand is still largely unnoticed and still working in mighty power.

It is unbecoming of us who are blessed by that hand not to notice. Busy in our routines, we sometimes forget that we are only instruments, tools. If we were really on our own, we "could not abound"—we could not succeed or grow (D&C 88:50; Alma 26:3). If Jesus needed his Father's help in order to do his Father's work, what does that say about us? (John 5:19; 15:5).

At the core of our feelings about life in the latter-day season is the trust we have in the constant presence of God's hand. Our faith drives out the countless worries and daily fears that are so common, and so expected, in the world.

After speaking to some Church members about this, Joseph Smith wrote in his journal: "I took occasion to gently reprove all present for letting report excite them, and advised them not to suffer themselves to be wrought upon by any report, but to maintain an even, undaunted mind."[68]

Ours is a day of reports. The latest news pummels the ear and the eye without mercy. But our faith filters each report through the "good news" that never changes, always applies, and is forever powerful in the mind.

New events may surprise us, but we know that the Lord is never surprised. No event can throw him off his great purposes. Whatever bad news comes along was already on his screen, for he "knoweth all things" (2 Nephi 2:24; 9:20; Mormon 8:22). We ourselves were ageless beings before the daily reports ever came rushing at us, and we will be pressing on through the eons long after the news has joined the dead and pointless dust of the past. To be "wrought upon" by passing report is to retreat from our treasured place at the side of our unruffled and steady Father, to abandon the gospel fortress of peace.

Joseph F. Smith counseled leaders to "never disseminate a spirit of gloom in the hearts of the people." He admitted that we might "feel the weight and anxiety of momentous times," but he taught that this should only prompt us to be "firmer and all the more resolute" in "the bright side of life rather than to permit its darkness and shadows to hover over" us.[69]

Our Father—whose hand is mighty, whose mind is even and undaunted, whose view is bright—will never cease to guide his latter-day people. It is our privilege to be that people.

71.
OUR MISSION
IS TO WIN

Talk about the Gentiles over-
whelming the Mormons and
destroying the work of God! Yes,
just as the Romans destroyed the
Jews and the Christians. I can go
out upon the street today and find
a Jew; I can go out and meet a
Christian; but has any one seen a
Roman of late? The Romans
became Christians, and the
Gentiles, tens of thousands of
them, perhaps millions, will
become Latter-day Saints.
—Orson F. Whitney[70]

History in progress can be a bit misleading. There were times when Judaism seemed to be fading from the great story of mankind. But on looking back, we discover that Jewish people survived and even took a major role in human progress, in all the sciences and arts. There was a time in the life of Jesus when some of his followers feared he had been defeated. But in his seeming loss he won the victory. He rose and still presides over all things and all people. Church history repeats the sweet plot of triumphs emerging from apparent disaster. In every nation, we will see this theme again and again.

One BYU sports fan put it this way: "If I miss the broadcast of a game, I try to watch the rebroadcast a couple of days later. In some ways, it isn't quite as exciting. By then I know who won; I've read about the key plays and final score. It's sort of funny, watching the fans and players and coaches worrying about a game you already know they're going to win. You want to say, 'Hey, settle down. Don't worry. Three plays from now you're going to get the ball back. In fact, it's going to be this particular player, and he's going to do it in this particular way. So just cheer up and go to work. You're going to win.'

"Of course, I can't say that to the images on the TV. They're not listening. But it's almost like that with the Lord. He knows how it's going to turn out. He knows all the players, all the key plays, and, of course, he knows the final score. If it ever looks like we're losing, he knows just when and how it's going to turn around. And we're not just shapes on a screen. We've heard his promises."

It's nice to cheer for a team you know is going to win. But it is far nicer to *be* on that team—to be a full member, a relentless contributor, a loyal and unwavering worker who never gets discouraged. The team doesn't need sympathetic spectators or fascinated fans. It needs workers. Through his servants, the Lord says to us, "Cheer up and go to work. You're going to win."

One such servant, Gordon B. Hinckley, has urged us, "Live by your standards. Pray for the guidance and protection of the Lord." He then promises, "He will never leave you alone. He will comfort you. He will sustain you. He will bless and magnify you and make your reward sweet and beautiful." Part of our reward will be drawing others in to these same blessings: "Your example will attract others who will take courage from your strength."[71]

Rome expired; Christianity lives on. We will win, and we will win souls. That is our mission.

72.
GETTING OUR WORK DONE

In an evil world we can so live our lives as to merit the protecting care of our Father in Heaven. . . . When the armaments of war ring out in deathly serenade and darkness and hatred reign in the hearts of some, there stands immovable, reassuring, comforting, and with great outreaching love the quiet figure of the Son of God.
—Gordon B. Hinckley[72]

The last days are proving dangerous for "the world." We are seeing the final days—the winding down, the closing era, the end—of all that is worldly, corrupt, and inhumane. But these are not the last days of righteousness. Our time is not dangerous for the righteous. Joseph B. Wirthlin described a house of faith as "a sanctuary where your family can be sheltered from the raging storms of life."[73] The gospel makes a home into both fortress and temple.

We are the people of him who rules all things. His Church is deliberately named and powerfully prepared for this era—not only for the dark and declining last days of the world but also for the magnificent *latter* days that include a millennium of increasing light. The latter days will not be crowded into a tight circle of mere safety but will expand in circles of saving. A dimming world cannot block Christ's power as it shines brighter. Circumstances ever so threatening will be safe to those who put themselves in his hands by their daily, deliberate decisions. That wise and safe approach brings to mind my friend Warren, a small, frail, elderly man of long experience. When we went to cut firewood I was young and new at it. We each brought our own truck and chainsaw. When Warren acted as if this would be a fun outing instead of grueling work, I worried that maybe he shouldn't be on such an errand.

Warren took forever to do things. Long after I began, I finally heard his saw start up. He worked only a short while and then stopped to move his truck. *Too old to carry the logs very far,* I realized. A few minutes later, he stopped again, this time to take his saw apart, clean it, and sharpen each tooth on the chain, one by one! *All the more reason for me to hurry,* I thought. *He'll be here all year unless I get done and help him.*

The morning waxed hot, and as my saw got dull, I bore down harder in order to get results. I glanced over and noticed Warren was taking another break—eating a slice of cake and drinking from a jug of ice water. That very jug was the one Warren used a short time later to dowse a fire I started. (My saw became so dull that it began burning its way through the logs.) Grateful I hadn't started the whole forest ablaze, I was surprised to see that Warren had somehow filled his truck bed, right up to the sideboards. Since my truck was less than half full, he was kind enough to sharpen my saw and help me finish. He seemed to enjoy it.

The urgency of our times must not rattle and rush us along. "The economy is struggling," Gordon B. Hinckley acknowledged. "There is conflict in the world. But the Almighty is keeping His promise that He will bless those who walk in faith and righteousness before Him."[74]

More than ever, we need to take time to stay spiritually fresh and sharp. If we do, we'll get through our work and enjoy it while we're at it.

73.
THE SPIRIT IS THE MASTER KEY

There is great safety as the young people of the Church accept the gospel. . . . There will be safety even in the times of great difficulty that are coming. There is a protection that they will have—because of the mighty change that has come in their hearts. They will choose righteousness and find that they have no more desire to do evil. That will come. It will not come in an instant, it will come over time.
—Henry B. Eyring[75]

The mighty change we read about in the scriptures is usually gradual. That is because it occurs in the human heart, where nothing can be remodeled without steady, ongoing consent, and because parallel growth must take its course in other departments of the soul. In other words, gradual is good. But if the change is not speedy, it is nevertheless mighty because of what is being changed. The invited Spirit of God actually alters what normally doesn't change at all—the very heart of our hopes and desires.

In the interesting years ahead, we will see a great wave of Latter-day Saints whose hearts will be refined by that wonderful change. This is just one of the reasons our day demands that we have the Spirit of the Lord with us.

Heber C. Kimball prophesied that further testing remained for the Saints in this dispensation, and he even told us the key for passing our tests: "To meet the difficulties that are coming, it will be necessary for you to have a knowledge of the truth of this work for yourselves. . . . The time will come when no man nor woman will be able to endure on borrowed light. Each will have to be guided by the light within himself."[76]

Henry B. Eyring reasoned clearly that the rock-solid kind of faith needed in our time "can only come through the witness of the Spirit." He advised teachers of the youth, "You must have the Spirit as your constant companion to teach with power, and your students will not survive spiritually without the Spirit as their companion."[77] Here again we see that our day is a special time for the gift of the Holy Ghost.

In urging us to use this wonderful aid, Boyd K. Packer cautioned, "I fear this supernal gift is being obscured. . . . There are so many places to go, so many things to do in this noisy world. We can be too busy to pay attention to the promptings of the Spirit." On the other hand, he gave this assurance: "We need not live in fear of the future. . . . If we follow the promptings of the Spirit, we will be safe, whatever the future holds. We will be shown what to do."[78]

No wonder Gordon B. Hinckley declared that "our safety lies in the virtue of our lives," for the Holy Ghost attends the pure.[79] Having the companionship of the Holy Ghost is like having a light to guide us through every latter-day shoal. Nothing can replace it; nothing can imitate it.

74.
BLESSED IN ALL THEY DO

Take a righteous course, brethren, and build up the kingdom of God, and all will be well with you continually, and all things will work together for your good.

—Heber C. Kimball [80]

As Alma described it, our baptismal covenant with God is that we "will serve him and keep his commandments" (Mosiah 18:10). In other words, ours is a covenant of worthiness and work, obedience and service, commandments and callings. Heber C. Kimball described this *dual* role by saying, "Take a righteous course, brethren, and build up the kingdom of God"— strength in *self* and strength in the *Church*. A faithful Latter-day Saint works at both. The blessings for doing so are almost unbelievable.

Alma says that God will "pour out his Spirit more abundantly upon you"—an ever-increasing gift (Mosiah 18:10). As we keep the twofold covenant yet another week and yet another year, the abundance is yet larger. The joy is greater, the guidance ever more sure and frequent, the fruit in personal strength and service to others even more sweet than the season before. The faithful who are old know even more about the goodness of God and the abundance of his Spirit than the faithful who are young.

Along with that mounting abundance, "all will be well with you continually," Heber C. Kimball said, "and all things will work together for your good." *All*—what a wide range! And yet that generous range is well known to those who make the will of God their quest and the work of God their mission. Heaven lavishes its partners with a generosity that never changes from generation to generation, age to age. King Benjamin said, "They are blessed in all things, both temporal and spiritual" (Mosiah 2:41; Romans 8:28; D&C 90:24).

A young couple in Tokyo had no sooner joined the Church than they strongly felt that Kotoku, the husband, should get an advanced degree at the university. This was not only unexpected but also financially impossible. But as soon as they set aside all their fears, they began to pray, not about whether to do it but about how to do it. One by one, doors opened. That was more than ten years ago, and it is clear from all the surprises since then that this one decision affected everything in their lives, the lives of their children, and numerous others they have served in the Church.

Joseph Smith said, "Abraham was guided in all his family affairs by the Lord; was conversed with by angels, and by the Lord; was told where to go, and when to stop; and prospered exceedingly in all that he put his hand unto; it was because he and his family obeyed the counsel of the Lord."[81]

So it is with all the covenant children of Abraham. In faith—trusting God's simple commandments—they do his will instead of their own. In faith—caring about God's purposes—they persist in his work despite the cost. Paul said that "they which are of faith, the same are the children of Abraham. . . . They which be of faith are blessed with faithful Abraham" (Galatians 3:7, 9). The God of Abraham sees to it that all is well with them.

75.
THE GREATEST WORK ON EARTH

Generations yet unborn will dwell with peculiar delight upon the scenes that we have passed through, . . . the all but insurmountable difficulties that we have overcome in laying the foundation of a work . . . that God and angels have contemplated with delight for generations past; . . . a work that is destined to bring about the destruction of the powers of darkness, the renovation of the earth, the glory of God, and the salvation of the human family.
—Joseph Smith[82]

Joseph Smith wore out his life. His companion, Emma, endured more than we can imagine. Brigham and his family willingly abandoned home after home. Pioneers pressed on through the taste of dust day after day. Handcart people, far from their European homes, collapsed upon their bedrolls in frozen, unfamiliar mountain passes at night. Those who lived to see another dawn did it again. After their odyssey on the bleak plains, the pioneers struck out on missions to create hundreds of settlements in the western wilderness. The first wave of workers in every nation labored, and labor now, in the face of enormous obstacles.

We of later waves have new obstacles. We hope to be as untiring as those who went before. Our "unwearyingness" swells the heart of our Heavenly Father and calls heavenly friends to our side (Helaman 10:4–5). Our "unwearyingness" invites them to "come down and join hand in hand in bringing about this work."[83]

Josef and Sylvia are citizens of a nation where the Church has only the merest footing so far. When they were baptized, they embraced the life of service. They stay in touch with Josef's home teaching families and Sylvia's visiting teaching sisters; they provide meals and transportation for the missionaries; they teach and lead week by week. Our Father's business is always on their minds, so they never lack for things to mention in prayer. In her clipped English, Sylvia says, "Our job you know is too big. But we pick out something each day and try. I don't know how, but the important part gets done." Josef adds, "It shouldn't go so well. We shouldn't be so blessed, but we are. Even our little boy, Soren, is happy when we are doing the greatest work on earth."

From an airplane on an overcast day, we discover a bright and blue sky above the clouds: there is no such thing as a sunless day. From the astronomer's telescope, we learn something about the night: there is not really a black expanse. Billions of stars fill the universe with shimmering silver. In the dome that weak eyes think is dark at night, all is ablaze with light.

They of the kingdom in heaven see what we of the kingdom on earth do not often see: there is no gray day or black night. When we do the work of the kingdom, we *feel* what they see. We feel that we are in the light, among friends, doing the greatest work on earth.

NOTES

1. Melvin J. Ballard, "Significance of South American Revolutions," *Improvement Era*, April 1931, 317.
2. David O. McKay, in Conference Reports of The Church of Jesus Christ of Latter-day Saints (Salt Lake City: The Church of Jesus Christ of Latter-day Saints, 1898 to present), April 1920, 116.
3. Joseph Smith, *History of The Church of Jesus Christ of Latter-day Saints,* ed. B. H. Roberts, 2d ed. rev., 7 vols. (Salt Lake City: The Church of Jesus Christ of Latter-day Saints, 1932–51), 4:609–10.
4. Henry B. Eyring, "A Child and a Disciple," *Ensign*, May 2003, 32.
5. Gordon B. Hinckley, "An Ensign to the Nations, a Light to the World," *Ensign,* November 2003, 84.
6. "The Living Christ: The Testimony of the Apostles," *Ensign*, April 2000, 2.
7. Spencer W. Kimball, "Let Us Move Forward and Upward," *Ensign,* May 1979, 82.
8. Gordon B. Hinckley, "Inspirational Thoughts," *Ensign,* August 2000, 5.
9. Gordon B. Hinckley, in "Messages of Inspiration from President Hinckley," *Church News,* 2 September 1995, 2.
10. Spencer W. Kimball, "When the World Will Be Converted," *Ensign,* October 1974, 14.
11. Gordon B. Hinckley, "Living in the Fulness of Times," *Ensign,* November 2001, 5.
12. Brigham Young, *Discourses of Brigham Young,* sel. John A. Widtsoe (Salt Lake City: Deseret Book, 1954), 130.
13. J. Reuben Clark Jr., "Constitution of the Restored Church and the Relationship of Its Members Thereto—The True Order of Priesthood," *Liahona, The Elders' Journal,* 13 March 1934, 461–62.
14. "Battle Hymn of the Republic," *Hymns of The Church of Jesus Christ of Latter-day Saints* (Salt Lake City: The Church of Jesus Christ of Latter-day Saints, 1985), no. 60. The original lyric, "Let us die," has been changed to "Let us live" in the hymnbook.
15. Joseph F. Smith, in Conference Report, October 1916, 154.
16. Anthony W. Ivins, in Conference Report, October 1928, 17.
17. Stephen L Richards, in Conference Report, October 1918, 66.
18. George Albert Smith, in Conference Report, October 1933, 26.
19. Adam S. Bennion, *The Candle of the Lord* (Salt Lake City: Deseret Book, 1958), 110.
20. Bruce R. McConkie, *The Millennial Messiah* (Salt Lake City: Deseret Book, 1982), 159.
21. Ibid., 170.
22. Ibid., 179.
23. Gordon B. Hinckley, "Living in the Fulness of Times," 6.

24. Spencer W. Kimball, *President Kimball Speaks Out* (Salt Lake City: Deseret Book, 1981), 96.
25. Joseph Smith, *History of the Church,* 4:540.
26. Gordon B. Hinckley, "An Ensign to the Nations, a Light to the World," 82.
27. Hugh B. Brown, "The Kingdom Is Rolling Forth," *Improvement Era,* December 1967, 93.
28. Joseph Smith, as cited by Heber C. Kimball, in *Journal of Discourses,* 26 vols. (London: Latter-day Saints' Book Depot, 1854–86), 3:263.
29. Richard G. Scott, "Finding Happiness," *Brigham Young University 1996–97 Speeches* (Provo, Utah: BYU Publications and Graphics, 1997), 364.
30. Gordon B. Hinckley, "The Church Goes Forward," *Ensign,* May 2002, 4.
31. Richard G. Scott, "The Power of a Strong Testimony," *Ensign,* November 2001, 88.
32. Robert D. Hales, "Faith through Tribulation Brings Peace and Joy," *Ensign,* May 2003, 18.
33. Gordon B. Hinckley, "The War We Are Winning," *Ensign,* November 1986, 44.
34. Wilford Woodruff, in *The Teachings of Ezra Taft Benson* (Salt Lake City: Bookcraft, 1988), 555.
35. Ezra Taft Benson, *The Teachings of Ezra Taft Benson,* 157.
36. Ezra Taft Benson, "Flooding the Earth with the Book of Mormon," *Ensign,* November 1988, 4.
37. Boyd K. Packer, "'The Standard of Truth Has Been Erected,'" *Ensign,* November 2003, 27.
38. Gordon B. Hinckley, "Inspirational Thoughts," 5.
39. Gordon B. Hinckley, in "Messages of Inspiration from President Hinckley," *Church News,* 7 December 1996, 2.
40. Henry B. Eyring, *To Draw Closer to God* (Salt Lake City: Deseret Book, 1997), 88.
41. George Albert Smith, *The Teachings of George Albert Smith* (Salt Lake City: Bookcraft, 1996), 146.
42. Henry B. Eyring, "An Enduring Testimony of the Mission of the Prophet Joseph," *Ensign,* November 2003, 91.
43. Gordon B. Hinckley, *Teachings of Gordon B. Hinckley* (Salt Lake City: Deseret Book, 1997), 356.
44. Joseph Smith, *Teachings of the Prophet Joseph Smith,* sel. Joseph Fielding Smith (Salt Lake City: Deseret Book, 1976), 112.
45. David O. McKay, in Conference Report, October 1959, 90.
46. Henry B. Eyring, "An Enduring Testimony of the Mission of the Prophet Joseph," 91.
47. Brigham Young, in *Wilford Woodruff's Journal,* ed. Scott G. Kenney, 9 vols. (Midvale, Utah: Signature Books, 1984), 5:384.
48. Thomas S. Monson, "To the Rescue," *Ensign,* May 2001, 50.
49. Henry B. Eyring, "An Enduring Testimony of the Mission of the Prophet Joseph," 92.

50. David O. McKay, "To Be in the Service of Our Fellowmen Is to Be in the Service of Our God," *Improvement Era,* December 1969, 87.

51. Thomas S. Monson, "Now Is the Time," *Ensign,* November 2001, 60.

52. Thomas S. Monson, "Stand in Your Appointed Place," *Ensign,* May 2003, 56.

53. James E. Faust, "These I Will Make My Leaders," *Ensign,* November 1980, 34–35.

54. John Young, in *Journal of Discourses,* 6:234.

55. Gordon B. Hinckley, in Carlos E. Asay, *The Seven M's of Missionary Service* (Salt Lake City: Bookcraft, 1996), 97.

56. David O. McKay, *Gospel Ideals* (Salt Lake City: Bookcraft, 1998), 332.

57. David O. McKay, *Man May Know for Himself* (Salt Lake City: Deseret Book, 1967), 108.

58. Dallin H. Oaks, "Repentance and Change," *Ensign,* November 2003, 38.

59. Ezra Taft Benson, "The Power of the Word," *Ensign,* May 1986, 82.

60. Hyrum Smith, in *History of the Church,* 6:323.

61. Henry B. Eyring, *We Must Raise Our Sights,* address to Church Educational System conference, Brigham Young University, 14 August 2001 (Salt Lake City: The Church of Jesus Christ of Latter-day Saints, 2001), 6.

62. Joseph Fielding Smith, *Doctrines of Salvation,* comp. Bruce R. McConkie, 3 vols. (Salt Lake City: Bookcraft, 1954–56), 1:311.

63. Howard W. Hunter, Church Educational System address, Temple Square Assembly Hall, 10 February 1989 (Salt Lake City: The Church of Jesus Christ of Latter-day Saints, 1989), 3.

64. Gordon B. Hinckley, "Your Greatest Challenge, Mother," *Ensign,* November 2000, 97.

65. David Whitmer, in B. H. Roberts, *A Comprehensive History of The Church of Jesus Christ of Latter-day Saints,* 6 vols. (Salt Lake City: The Church of Jesus Christ of Latter-day Saints, 1965), 1:131.

66. George Q. Cannon, in *Collected Discourses,* comp. Brian H. Stuy, 5 vols. (Burbank, Calif.: B.H.S. Publishing, 1987–92), 4:305.

67. Joseph F. Smith, *Gospel Doctrine* (Salt Lake City: Deseret Book, 1975), 52.

68. Joseph Smith, *History of the Church,* 5:98.

69. Joseph F. Smith, *Gospel Doctrine,* 155.

70. Orson F. Whitney, in Conference Report, October 1910, 53.

71. Gordon B. Hinckley, "An Ensign to the Nations, a Light to the World," 84.

72. Gordon B. Hinckley, "War and Peace," *Ensign,* May 2003, 81.

73. Joseph B. Wirthlin, *Finding Peace in Our Lives* (Salt Lake City: Deseret Book, 1995), 58.

74. Gordon B. Hinckley, "The Condition of the Church," *Ensign,* May 2003, 6.

75. Henry B. Eyring, "We Must Raise Our Sights," 6.

76. Heber C. Kimball, cited by Harold B. Lee, in Conference Report, October 1965, 128.

77. Henry B. Eyring, "A Challenging Time—A Wonderful Time," Church Educational System address, Salt Lake Tabernacle, 7 February 2003 (Salt Lake City: The Church of Jesus Christ of Latter-day Saints, 2003), 1.

78. Boyd K. Packer, "The Cloven Tongues of Fire," *Ensign*, May 2000, 8.

79. Gordon B. Hinckley, "'Till We Meet Again,'" *Ensign*, November 2001, 90.

80. Heber C. Kimball, in *Journal of Discourses*, 6:325.

81. Joseph Smith, *Teachings of the Prophet Joseph Smith*, 251–52.

82. Ibid., 232.

83. Ibid., 159.

Part D
Promises for the Afterlife

When we have lived long enough . . . to see the least Saint, that can be possibly called a Saint, in possession of more solar systems like this, than it is possible for mortals to number, or than there are stars in the firmament of heaven visible, or sands on the sea shore, we shall then have a faint idea of eternity, and begin to realize that we are in the midst of it. —Brigham Young[1]

Latter-day prophets have pointed out a safe and godly path through the everyday mortal world. But they have also delivered promises about another world, an immortal one, a transcendent one. As we shall see in the last pages of this book, they have made promise after promise that we will someday transcend the life we are now living. Now and then they invite us to raise our sights from daily blessings to the incredible glories just ahead.

76.
SURROUNDED BY FRIENDS

Do we realize that in our daily walk and work we are not alone, but that angels attend us wherever our duty causes us to go? It is only when we stray into unholy places, only when we tread upon forbidden ground, that they leave us to ourselves; and then they watch us from the distance with sorrow and tears. Those holy beings think it not beneath their state to abide in the hovels of the poor, to stand by us in the most menial labor, provided it be honorable employment.

—James E. Talmage[2]

The hosts of heaven don't have to drop all their other work just to tend to us all the time. Divine guidance works more efficiently and personally than that. Our Father, ministering through the Holy Ghost, is not dependent upon a staff of countless middlemen.

However, the care of the Godhead—the attention of the Father, the Son, and the Holy Ghost to our lives—does not prevent the hosts of heaven from caring, knowing, and watching. They may be assigned as messengers or helpers, as agents of the Holy Ghost, just as people in the flesh are frequently instruments in the hands of God, inspired by the Holy Ghost to help their fellow mortals. Under the presiding love and power of God, we have added friends who have love and power. At times, and most especially when we are being good and doing good, worthy ones of the other world join in our efforts. The great work of the kingdom, which knows no boundaries, is theirs as well as ours, ours as well as theirs.

Why, then, do we not notice them? For the same reason that the divine members of the Godhead also escape our notice. Elder Talmage said, "Our eyes are so heavy, our ears so dull, that we see and hear only the things of earth."[3] Some of our deafness and blindness comes of being caught up with ourselves—our unbelieving opinions and unimportant ambitions. And yet, as long as we live in mortality, we will be largely unaware of nonmortal realities.

Those realities aren't far away. "We move and have our being in the presence of heavenly messengers and of heavenly beings," said Joseph F. Smith. Those beings once walked on our terrain and have moved on to other, more interesting scenes. Looking back as if through a one-way window, they are endowed with mounting wisdom. They possess stronger and more refined feelings. President Smith continued, "They have advanced; we are advancing; we are growing as they have grown. . . . They love us now more than ever. . . . Their solicitude for us, and their love for us, and their desire for our well being, must be greater than that which we feel for ourselves."[4]

It may be that we have many more good friends in that world than we do in this world. So how do we align ourselves with them? How do we become worthy of their attentions? The standard is always the same. "I promise you," said L. Tom Perry, "if you will heed the voice of warning of the Holy Ghost and will follow His direction, you will be blessed with the ministering of angels, which will add wisdom, knowledge, power, and glory to your life."[5]

The Holy Ghost is the ultimate guardian angel. If we hearken to his promptings—the daily urgings to be good and do good—we will be surrounded by friends.

77.
EACH SOUL IS TREASURED

There is not one of us but what God's love has been expended upon. There is not one of us that He has not cared for and caressed. There is not one of us that He has not desired to save, and that He has not devised means to save. There is not one of us that He has not given His angels charge concerning. . . . The truth remains that we are the children of God, and that He has actually given His angels—invisible beings of power and might—charge concerning us, and they watch over us and have us in their keeping.
—George Q. Cannon[6]

On one occasion, the disciples of Jesus were looking at some nearby children, children typical of any time and place, perhaps a little loud and undisciplined, perhaps soiled from their playing on the dusty paths of their neighborhood. Suddenly the disciples heard a comment from Jesus, a caution: "Take heed that ye despise not one of these little ones; for I say unto you, that in heaven their angels do always behold the face of my Father which is in heaven" (Matthew 18:10). At this moment, they and we are watched by eyes that are wiser, more realistic, more perceptive, and more charitable than our own.

When we are invited to obtain the pure love of Christ, we are given a list of symptoms to watch for: "charity suffereth long, and is kind, and envieth not, and is not puffed up, seeketh not her own, is not easily provoked, thinketh no evil, and rejoiceth not in iniquity but rejoiceth in the truth, beareth all things, believeth all things, hopeth all things, endureth all things" (Moroni 7:45; 1 Corinthians 13:4–7).

Of course, these characteristics are perfected in Jesus. He suffers long, meaning that he is exceedingly patient with us. He is always kind in the core of his feelings for us. Never does a hint of envy pass through his heart. The list is a brief and modest description of the way he is inside.

The more fully developed followers of Christ are, the more fully they possess those same traits. Our friends who live in the spirit world view us patiently, kindly, respectfully. They treasure us, not simply because they are so nice but also because they are in full contact with reality. They treasure us because we are real treasures. They love us because we are really loveable. If we have trouble loving the mortals around us, or if we have trouble loving ourselves, the problem lies in us, in our immature hearts and unseeing eyes.

The abandoned child, the battered wife, the unvisited patient in a care center—these are actually the children of royalty. Higher beings know it and never forget it. The little boy who has low scores in school and carping adults at home is convinced that he has no value. But in heaven he is always honored, as is the abused little girl whose life is a round of nightmares. She supposes she is worthless and dirty. But angels know the glorious truth about her and her redeemed future. Her path to joy has already been planned. Hosts of heaven will host her there in due time. The day of her surprise is on the calendar. The love of Christ, burning in angelic hearts, will be poured out in its season on every soul. The treasures will all be known.

78.
MOVING US TO ACTION

The Prophet Joseph, the twelve apostles, with many of the elders of Israel and saints have been called to pass through scenes of suffering and privation that would have discouraged an Alexander. They have had to combat earth and hell, wicked men and devils, sickness and death, burnings, drivings and persecutions. But have we been discouraged? No. The greater the difficulties the more we have been stimulated to Action.

—Wilford Woodruff [7]

To a particular family one evening, word came of a foul event, an insulting deed against one of the family members. Jason, an older brother, was inflamed at the news. In rage he stormed to the door, vowing to take revenge. The family had just been shocked in one way, and now Jason was shocking them in another. But then came another surprise. Mild-mannered Andrew, a four-year-old, ran to the door and blocked Jason's path.

"Out of my way," yelled Jason. "No," Andrew answered with nostrils flaring, "not till we pray." When Jason tried to move Andrew to the side and swing the door open, Andrew dove through Jason's reach and wrapped his little arms around one of Jason's knees, clamping his teeth onto the pant leg. Jason dragged his leg and his little brother out into the front yard but finally stopped. Anger was suspended by a special kind of courage, the moral courage of love. Soon, with the smallest family member still attached to the biggest, the whole family was at Jason's side. They all reentered the house, where they would council together about their new challenge.

Courage can, and usually does, transfer from one person to another. Bravery spreads between soldiers on fields of mortal danger. It spreads in workplaces and on teams. Firmness rubs off of heroes we haven't even met. Many a bedridden patient, awaiting the next step in some medical ordeal, has found new resolve in the mere presence of a loving visitor. Likewise, we may be transformed by beings we do not know and cannot see. As the Lord predicted, they will be "round about you, to bear you up" (D&C 84:88). Their nearness makes a difference. With power they bear us up, stimulating us to Action with a capital "A," as Wilford Woodruff spelled it. Perhaps little Andrew was so decisive because of love and firmness pouring into him through the veil.

As the love of a small boy gave moral courage to a big boy, our unseen friends bear us up by their pure love. As John the Beloved said, "Perfect love casteth out fear" (1 John 4:18), or, as Mormon said, "all fear" (Moroni 8:16).

Along with purer love, those beings have gone on to mightier faith. Just as we mortals strengthen each other by bearing testimony, they can instill faith in our hearts. Like love, faith dispels fear.

If we try to follow Jesus—praying without fail, tithing without fail, fulfilling our callings without fail—we have the nearness of him who is firm without fail (D&C 112:19). Then we can face anything. He and the courageous hosts of heaven, by their nearness, move us to Action.

79.
WE WILL DO A GREAT DEAL MORE

Our beloved brother Brigham Young has gone from us, to join the Prophet Joseph and the host of the holy and the pure who are behind the veil; but we do not therefore lose the benefit of his labors. He is now in a position to do more for that work.

—John Taylor[8]

For the faithful who die, privileges expand. One of these privileges is assisting the people they left behind. As with Brigham Young when he died, we may prove more helpful there than we are here.

In fact, Brigham Young said so at the funeral of one of his counselors, Jedediah M. Grant. From his remarks we learn several wonderful things. For example, he said, "Brother Grant can now do ten times more than if he was in the flesh."[9] Jedediah M. Grant was a doer, a teacher, and a leader of enormous influence. And yet, his capacity was multiplied beyond the veil. To be liberated, to be effective and almost limitless in our service, would be more than thrilling. What a promise!

And how does this multiplying take place? "He is no more subject to the devils that dwell in the infernal regions; he commands them, and they must go at his bidding; he can move them just as I can move my hand."

One reason for coming into this world was to face evil on its home court and yet to give no heed to its enticements. If we come out of this test in cleanness, we don't have to take the test again. We do not go on forever ducking and weaving defensively, narrowly avoiding the traps of the adversary. When Jedediah M. Grant went hence, Satan's hosts lost every shred of dominion they once held over him. So it is with every righteous man or woman.

"When men overcome as our faithful brethren have," Brigham explained, they "go where they see Joseph, who will dictate [to] them and be their head and Prophet all the time." We will enjoy our privileges and adventures in that world in close partnership with earth's greatest heroes—all without Satan's pesky intrusions. Leading our way will be Joseph Smith. We will count him and other nobles as our friends and companions.

Of course, we do not want to leave mortal life prematurely. We want to enter the next phase after we have finished all our work here and not an hour sooner. But when the time is right to move on, the next step should hold no horror for us. "The spirit is unlocked from the body," as Brigham described the moment. Until that liberation, we are in a battle, an ongoing and daily struggle, because "you and I have yet to deal with evil spirits." But for the righteous, mortal death ends the struggle and brings personal victory over the forces of evil. Then, "when the spirit is unlocked from the tabernacle it is as free, pure, holy, and independent of them as the sun is of this earth."

Thus, President Young could say of his former counselor, "I have not felt, for one minute, that Jedediah is dead." And what is true of Jedediah M. Grant applies to all who live the gospel fulness. For them, life doesn't just go on; it expands. When it comes to real success—true service, rewarding growth, and a fulness of joy—"there we will do a great deal more than we can here."

80.
COOPERATION ACROSS THE VEIL

The servants of God who have lived on the earth in ages past will reveal where different persons have lived who have died without the Gospel, give their names, and say, "Now go forth, ye servants of God, and exercise your rights and privileges; go and perform the ordinances of the house of God for those who have passed their probation without the law, and for all who will receive any kind of salvation: bring them up to inherit the celestial, terrestrial, and telestial kingdoms."
—Brigham Young[10]

To perform an ordinance for someone who doesn't live here anymore, we have to know just enough to distinguish her from everyone else. For example, if we don't know when and where a certain person named Katherine lived, we can't be certain which of earth's many Katherines she is. We want to offer her the ordinances of baptism and confirmation and the gift of the Holy Ghost. We want to seal her to her parents, her husband, and her children.

But once we have done that and then learn about another Katherine, how can we keep track of the two, and how will each Katherine know when it is her particular work that is being done? By other details besides her name, such as her birth, marriage, or death. No other Katherine was born at her time and her place and to her parents.

Unfortunately, many Katherines and other souls have come through the mortal doors and gone out again, unnoticed in the records of mankind. Or if a record was made, it may now be lost. In those cases, Church policy permits us to do the ordinance if we have a telling clue, such as the names of other family members. But that still leaves billions in the spirit world who left no trail.

Those souls are so important that the normal silence and subtlety of heaven must be broken. Some of the most anonymous people in all history will be the subjects of divine revelation! "The Priesthood behind the veil," John Taylor assured us, will "communicate with the Priesthood upon the earth."[11] Heavenly beings will bring crucial information, millennial mortals will go ahead with ordinances, and individuals will be free to accept their own covenants personally and privately in the house of the Lord.

Resurrected beings will visit the earth and join in the work with faithful people living during the Millennium. Will they be on hand constantly? Joseph Fielding Smith wrote that these beings "shall not remain here all the time during the thousand years, but they will mingle with those who are still here in mortal life." That they will "mingle" suggests friendship, contact, and joint effort with their earth-bound partners. They will shed light on gospel principles, bring information regarding the dead, jointly discuss the living and dead who are in need, and attend conferences and other meetings.

On one hand will be "these resurrected saints and the Saviour Himself," and on the other hand will be the privileged mortals that host them.[12] Whether we are among the mortals or immortals of that period hardly matters, for all will rejoice in their role. What matters is that we are included in those sacred experiences, important successes, and happy associations. Now is our opportunity to prove worthy to work in that day.

81.
GREATER SUCCESS IN TEACHING

A wonderful work is being accomplished in our temples in favor of the spirits in prison. I believe, strongly too, that when the Gospel is preached to the spirits in prison, the success attending that preaching will be far greater than that attending the preaching of our Elders in this life. I believe there will be very few indeed of those spirits who will not gladly receive the Gospel when it is carried to them. The circumstances there will be a thousand times more favorable.

—Lorenzo Snow[13]

A missionary couple wrote the following to a grandson, who was about to leave for his own mission: "In your letter you asked if it is hard teaching people the gospel. We have discussed your question for several days, and we keep coming up with the same answer. It's hard when people don't care. On the other hand, it's a great joy to teach the ones who care so much that they are hungering for truth. As Jesus said, 'Blessed are all they who do hunger and thirst after righteousness, for they shall be filled with the Holy Ghost' (3 Nephi 12:6).

"Matt, that's really how it is, whether you are teaching members or nonmembers. The teacher who cares about the will of the Father more than anything else will be filled with the Holy Ghost. Same with the student or investigator. That's one thing we've learned for sure. You don't always have hungry people to teach. But when you do, you'll notice the difference. It will take everything you've got, but it won't be hard."

That couple made one of the most important discoveries in our Father's great kingdom: the Lord never turns away anyone who is hungry. But it is true that he may let the complacent person go without a meal. When students are quite satisfied with themselves, or when the teacher feels little need for inspiration, the inspiration may not come. When we thirst after the Spirit, when we want mightily to be better and wiser, we will find ourselves filled.

When President Snow spoke of "circumstances" being a thousand times better in the spirit world, he meant more than nice chairs and good lighting. We can hardly imagine how splendid it is to meet in the spirit world with people who have been waiting hundreds of years for the truth. They have grown up emotionally since their shortsighted years on earth. They have progressed from mere curiosity to aching desire. They have long pondered their questions and exhausted other sources. They—billions of them—want a true messenger.

People pass into mortality by birth and then pass out of it in a few years, a handful of decades. Great throngs of souls leaving mortal life pour into the spirit world without a break, day or night. Theirs numbers are staggering, for they accumulate. They don't move on until the day of resurrection. "The elders of Israel and the Saints of God in the spirit world," said Wilford Woodruff, "have all the spirits who have lived on the earth. . . . They are shut up in prison, awaiting the message of the Elders of Israel."[14]

It is good to know that they are "awaiting the message." It is exciting to consider the vast number of spiritual experiences still ahead for us. And it is wonderful beyond words to know that those waiting nations will "gladly receive the Gospel," just as we will gladly impart it.

82.
REMOVING THE STING

If you want to have a glorious end to your life, to robe immortality about you, and to lie down to sweet rest with a hope, with joy in your heart, do something for your kindred dead, and I promise you that you will take the sting of death out of your hearts. You will fill the last days of your life with joy and happiness, and you will be building for your eternal joy and happiness.

—Melvin J. Ballard[15]

Imagine a brave journey, one of many stings and stages, leading at last to the splendid house of a renowned and beloved king. No pilgrim will reach this destination except by loyalty to the king all along and by diligence proven again and again. For that reason, each new arrival is received at the king's door by respectful hosts, who at some time long since made this same journey themselves. Their acquaintance with the king and their devotion to him is evident as they work about the mansion. To associate with them is to have some hint about meeting the king in person. And surely not long after entering his house that privilege will come. The stings are all gone.

The destination is ours. And the King is our king. But first the journey. We start out hardly awake, and so small—physically and spiritually. We then pass through a spring of experimenting and exploring. Given time, we awaken. And ever so slowly we grow. We grow at about the speed of a tree. Any one change is too small to see with the naked eye. Only when the changes combine over a long time do we realize that we are growing.

Then comes the summer of long days and hard work to stand on our own feet in the world. Experience gives way to wisdom—long-needed, long-awaited. When the time is right we build a celestial marriage, which takes more patience and unselfishness than we could have known. And it may be our privilege during our lengthy summer to rear children. It will take every available hour and every available dollar for two decades or so. That will be three or four decades if there are many children in our home. When summer is passed, we are not so small anymore.

Before the winter can still our journey, before we enter the world of spirits and know the end of tests and the beginning of rest, we may be granted an autumn. We may serve a mission or two. With delight and some surprise, we harvest the golden growth that came to us since spring.

Autumn may even permit time for yet another service before graduating to the spirit world—a labor flavored with the taste of heaven. We may be hosts in the house of the King. Our life may be crowned with another sort of adventure, this one quiet and white in the presence of angels. We have been patient with each season, and only now in the temple do we sometimes see where it was we were heading all along. In the temple, that glimpse removes the sting of death.

Within temple doors, we set prisoners free. We break off chains and then create unbreakable chains that link people who are dear to each other. We extend the sealing power by extending ourselves in the temple, and in the process we extend families. In the last season of mortal life, we are covered with joy, for we know the King is watching our service in his house. We are doing as he does. We know he approves. We know his kind of joy. At last, we are coming to know him.

83.
THE ULTIMATE FAMILY BUSINESS

A brother reached out his hand, a brother eighty years of age and upwards. . . . I recognized him as a man who had been much in the temple here, and I said to the party sitting next to him, "This is a temple man," and the brother spoke up and said, "Yes, Brother Clawson, I have officiated in the temple for twelve hundred souls." Then I turned again to the party next to him and said: "Our brother here may pass through life unnoticed; he may attract but little attention, but I tell you he will be a big man in the other world."
—Rudger Clawson[16]

The reward to the "temple man" is not a promise of fame. It is a promise of appreciation and more—eternal gratitude. He could have spent those long hours in leisure. Or he might have spent them in some service that can be measured by the natural eye or the natural mind. Instead, he gave those hours through absolute faith in Christ, a gift to the salvation process God has ordained. In partnership with Christ, that man gave life's premiere commodities—time, self, attention. He donated himself to the ultimate business. His gift will never be forgotten by the souls he served.

We knew them all in person during our long premortal life. We will get reacquainted someday. But during mortal time we know but a tiny fraction of our former and future loved ones. To search out a few definite things about the families that came before us is no casual task. Even if someone else does the searching and organizing for us, the information has to be grasped in the heart. Only love can transform a bit of data into a loved one. Getting approval for ordinances, carrying that information to the temple, and transforming eternity for a loved one are not jobs for the selfish or worldly heart. They are works of love.

We expect to be in eternal families, but that future comes at some price—the price of caring. The people who can best measure that future—and who can tell us the worth of the modest, earthy data we need to do the work—are the recipients. The experts are those we serve when we act on that data. Their timeless gratitude tells it all.

Another measure of this business—the family creation business that operates in our Father's house—was suggested by Heber J. Grant: "To a Latter-day Saint a book of this size [holding up the Book of Mormon], containing the names of his ancestors, is worth many, many times, hundreds of times more than its weight in gold."[17]

Suppose you reach out and take up a binder full of family research. On its pages are written names and places, dates and sources, relationships and ordinances. Suppose you hold sixteen ounces of data in your hands—worth more than six thousand dollars if the record were in gold, but worth millions by Heber J. Grant's calculation of "hundreds of times more than its weight in gold." The book in your hands documents a network of loved ones that will transcend time and gold—creating and using it is a holy family business that will include you when you leave this world.

No matter what it costs to find that information and act on it with your heart and your strength, it will prove to be a bargain.

84.
ETERNAL INCREASE OF JOY

Let me here say a word to console the feelings and hearts of all who belong to this Church. Many of the sisters grieve because they are not blessed with offspring. You will see the time when you will have millions of children around you. If you are faithful to your covenants, you will be mothers of nations. . . . Be faithful and if you are not blessed with children in this time, you will be hereafter.

—Brigham Young[18]

One Saturday afternoon my son and I had one of those unforgettable moments. While out on an errand, we both had an impulse to stop at the Berrett home, where we had been home teaching only a few days before. We enjoyed this family, with their eleven fun-loving children and their healthy gospel attitude. But this hardly seemed the time for a casual visit. We had two surprises when Sister Berrett answered the door: she was the only one home, and she was in tears. "Is there something wrong?" I asked with my typical brilliance.

"Not really, I guess," she answered awkwardly as the three of us stood together in the entryway. "It's just that . . . for twenty-three years or so I've always had a baby. Sometimes when I'm alone, I get thinking about that." There was a pause while she looked at the floor and tears began to well up again. "And I have to face up to it. Those days are gone—forever."

"Sister Bennett," I said, "those days are not gone forever. You know that, don't you?" She raised her head and asked, "I do?"

She did know that in a way. But somehow she had not noticed how the doctrine of exaltation applied to her instinctive love of new life. In our next visit to that home, we reminded her of what Joseph Smith declared. Worthy couples "will continue to increase and have children in the celestial glory."[19] Earth life is not the end of our child-bearing career. It is only the beginning.

All the righteous eventually feel the same way. They want the springs of eternity to renew the old lives and old relationships forever, but at the same time they will always long for new lives to begin. Mothers sometimes call it "baby hunger." The Lord's answer to that natural and holy wish is what he calls "increase," or "eternal lives" (D&C 131:4; 132:24).

"It is the blessed privilege of resurrected beings who attain an exaltation in the celestial kingdom," James E. Talmage said, "to enjoy the glory of endless increase, to become the parents of generations of spirit-offspring." What will exalted parents then do for those offspring? They will "direct their development through probationary stages analogous to those through which they themselves have passed."[20]

Our fondness for little ones is not just linked to the delight of holding an innocent life or to the privilege of creating that life. Sister Bennett, and each who receives what the Father hath, will inherit his work in a realm where pain and tedium are no more. She will embrace and nurture and elevate lives forever. And with every new life, she will have an increase of joy.

85.
ALL WILL KNOW

Sometime, somewhere, the knowledge of the Lord shall come to every soul with saving or convicting effect; then every knee shall bow, and every tongue confess that He is the Christ, the Son of the Living God.

—James E. Talmage[21]

You are driving through a neighborhood and notice a little boy who has climbed part way out of his house. He was creative enough to go out the window head-first and is now hanging from the opening. He cannot climb back in, and it has dawned on him that dropping headfirst would not be smart. He is crying, and time is running out. You quickly stop your car and run through the front gate to his rescue. You walk him to the front door and explain matters to his grateful parent.

A larger plot just like that unfolds, or ought to unfold, in the story of every life. We are minding our own business—our slightly unimportant or self-centered business—and suddenly learn of some noble opportunity or important power. A gate opens to us. We have a hero's decision to make. *Will we choose that gate or ignore it?* If we do the heroic thing, we are led on to new gates, new paths, new opportunities. If we refrain, we never pass through those other gates. We never see them or know about them.

We sing that "they who reject this glad message shall never such happiness know."[22] From those who refrain from the gate of baptism, for example, celestial scenes will be forever withheld. They can see the symptoms of peace in Christian lives but do not feel it themselves. A thousand other blessings escape their narrow experience.

All people will someday know for sure that the gate truly was their golden opportunity. They will know beyond doubt that it was the heroic choice. Those who now seem so uninterested or disdainful toward gospel treasures will someday change their opinion. They will crave to touch the treasure and will want to align themselves with the truth in every possible way. They will rejoice in contemplating what they know of it, even as the faithful joy in it now. They will honor him whom the faithful honored all along.

Perhaps when you stopped your car and ran through the gate to that little boy's rescue, a driver behind you complained impatiently or made fun. This person misunderstood the situation or perhaps understood and yet resented your choice. But it didn't matter. You did not waste time feeling picked on. Heroes give no heed to their critics, as Lehi said of the righteous in his dream (1 Nephi 8:33–34; D&C 20:22).

Joseph Smith understood, from the First Vision to his martyrdom, that his enemies did not understand. Our missionaries know that some of their investigators will not acknowledge the truth for a long time, but as good heroes they go on loving, teaching, and imploring.

Jesus was aware that those who brutalized him would someday apologize (Mosiah 27:30–31). But he never gloated and will not gloat in that day of universal humility. We won't gloat either, and we must not gloat now. Our job is to love people as they will be when their eyes are opened.

86.
OUR PATH FOREVER

What you have to do is get on the straight and narrow path—thus charting a course leading to eternal life—and then, being on that path, pass out of this life in full fellowship. . . . If you're on that path and pressing forward, and you die, you'll never get off the path. There is no such thing as falling off the straight and narrow path in the life to come.
—Bruce R. McConkie[23]

In mercy, those who are not faithful in this life may be given time to advance further in the spirit world. But it is also merciful that those who are faithful don't have to start over when they leave here. Somehow our Father has designed the mortal test so that enough is enough.

The narrow path is not hard to understand. There isn't a mysterious list of extra demands, no secret club of elite Saints. The scriptures tell us all about the pure heart, and Church leaders often demonstrate by their deeds what that means in case we have any doubt. We cannot hold a temple recommend without an interview that makes the standard perfectly clear. The covenants we make in the temple are spelled out in simple language.

If we have not reached the end of the path, at least we are on it. But are we doing our best to press forward, or are we stepping off now and then for unworthy diversions? Each person knows the answer. Why are we expected to answer for ourselves in a recommend interview? Because we are quite able to detect whether we are on the path of salvation.

You can drive your car east from the balmy gold and green hills of California, travel the high desert of Nevada, the even higher Rocky Mountains, and never stop until you have passed the vast corn country of Nebraska. You'll then pass more freight trucks than you ever thought possible on the outskirts of Chicago and, skirting the Great Lakes, end up crossing the Hackensack River in New Jersey. You can travel these three thousand miles without ever leaving Interstate Highway 80.

Scenic perhaps, but oh what scenery the path of salvation passes! What marvelous heights are guaranteed that traveler who never leaves this route. Bruce R. McConkie's statement reminds us that the path crosses not only through this world but also the spirit world. It is the most adventurous route in the universe, the one road that will be known to all noble men and women.

In fact, once we have reached exaltation, we will continue on this road forever. Even now, in the beginning miles, the culture of this straight journey tells us a lot about where we are going. We will always live worthily, we will always be strictly honest, pure, kind, and happy. We need only get started and be settled and steady in this road. We need only stay on it to the end of our brief probation, and it will be our highway through the galaxies forever.

87.
ULTIMATE RELIEF

We shall turn round and look upon [the valley of death] and think, when we have crossed it, why this is the greatest advantage of my whole existence, for I have passed from a state of sorrow, grief, mourning, woe, misery, pain, anguish and disappointment into a state of existence, where I can enjoy life to the fullest extent as far as that can be done without a body.

—Brigham Young[24]

Every day finds Sohah at her place on the sidewalk of a particular street in the shopping district of Amman, Jordan. In the terms of some who see her, this young lady of twenty-one years is a beggar. Her distorted frame, formed to accommodate her unshifting posture the past fifteen years, is full of maladies. Sohah is in perpetual discomfort. She cannot with her eyes see any of those who drop small change onto her worn wool blanket, but should you stop and look into those eyes, you will find them full of patience and contrition. Her few joys come at late evening with her aging mother, who is also blind, in the tiny shelter they call home along a nearby alley.

When we consider how many of mankind travel upstream in daily tribulation, it seems that Sohah's hard existence is not rare. Billions of our siblings battle simply to survive each day. No other life is quite understandable to them. Their circumstances seem forever cursed with shortages of some kind. Or they know constant disability. Or they chafe under the tight hold of political leaders with narrow minds and hardened hearts.

These all find that life is like a climb through desolate hills and cannot know what it is to rest in the shadows of a peaceful meadow or to glide down a gentle slope. It hardly matters whether we speak of actual shadows and slopes or symbolic ones. Not many of our fellow beings know relief.

They are in for a great surprise. The world we live in now is no fair sample of the long and recent and luxurious existence we have all forgotten and which will resume in the near future. Dreariness, though it serves a purpose, is the extravagant exception. It is momentary. Luxury is the rule. It is eternal. The mortal moment is a purposely altered event, weighed down with tears and trouble. Here we find beauty but little of it compared to the norm of eternity. Here we see occasional genius but not constant and full as is the norm for our Father's children when they are not fettered by mortal brains and bodies.

As Brigham Young assures us, when we finish our duties here we will, with wonder and awe, leave behind all of our burdens of misery and woe. We will never pick them up again. Sohah will be stunned with joy. Likewise Della, a mother who spent all of her adult days and waking hours caring for an autistic daughter. Sohah and Della, and you and I, will be filled with relief immeasurable, with surprise unequaled, and with worship inexpressible.

88.

JOY IN CHRIST

I testify to you this day that the time will come when every man, woman, and child will look into the Savior's loving eyes. On that day, we will know with a surety the worth of our decision to straightway follow Him.
—Joseph B. Wirthlin[25]

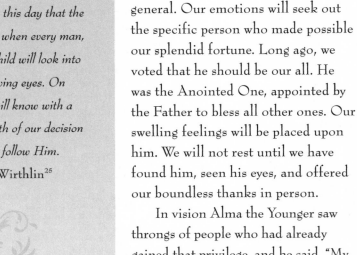

Surprise and relief, joy and comfort, thanksgiving and worship —these will fill us on passing through the doorway of death. It will not be joy unfocused or worship in general. Our emotions will seek out the specific person who made possible our splendid fortune. Long ago, we voted that he should be our all. He was the Anointed One, appointed by the Father to bless all other ones. Our swelling feelings will be placed upon him. We will not rest until we have found him, seen his eyes, and offered our boundless thanks in person.

In vision Alma the Younger saw throngs of people who had already gained that privilege, and he said, "My soul did long to be there" (Alma 36:22). Now his soul is there. In time our souls will be there too. The doctrine of rejoicing in Christ is not a frilly daydream. When the prophets bring it up, they speak of it in all seriousness (Philippians 3:3; Psalm 33:21; 2 Nephi 25:26). As Elder Wirthlin testified, everyone "will look into the Savior's loving eyes."

In that never-forgettable moment, we will find that "intelligence cleaveth unto intelligence; wisdom receiveth wisdom; truth embraceth truth; virtue loveth virtue; light cleaveth unto light" (D&C 88:40). That is, we will immediately know if our spirit is compatible with his. If we don't belong there with him, no one will have to force that fact upon us. Sad and forlorn will be those who leave his presence to live on in lesser glory (D&C 76:75–82; 88:21–23).

A visionary experience of Melvin J. Ballard only hints at the joy of those who do not have to depart from him in that day. After seeing and embracing Jesus for but a moment, Elder Ballard said, "The feeling that I had in the presence of him who hath all things in his hands, to have his love, his affection, and his blessing was such that if I ever can receive that of which I had but a foretaste, I would give all that I am, all that I ever hope to be, to feel what I then felt!"[26]

The personal love of the Savior is one thing to hear about or imagine, another thing to experience in his presence. Once we have actually seen the patient focus of his eye upon us, once we have witnessed his smile approving and enveloping and renewing our personal life, once the strong tide of his light has flowed from his own being into ours, we will long as Alma did: to have it so always.

In the hours of their difficulty, early Church members were assured by the Prophet Joseph Smith, "The mind is led to rejoice amid all its trials and temptations, in hope of that glory which is to be brought at the revelation of Jesus Christ." Even now we can rejoice in that day of days, "in view of that crown which is to be placed upon the heads of the saints, . . . when he shall bring them in the midst of his throne to dwell in his presence eternally."[27]

But a few efforts and a few moments more, and that day will be ours.

89.
BEAUTY AND JOY

My hopes in reference to the future life are supremely grand and glorious, and I try to keep these prospects bright continually; and that is the privilege and the duty of every Latter-day Saint.

—Lorenzo Snow[28]

We don't have all the mental tools just now to comprehend the joy and beauty that lie ahead. But to go with our hopes we have clues, and it is good to keep those clues "bright continually."

Just as a child might run her hand over the mysterious shape of a wrapped birthday present, we have some big hints. One clue, for example, is a happy home life. Thomas S. Monson declared, "To hear the laughter of children, to witness the expression of love by parents, and to feel the embrace of brothers and sisters provide a preview of heaven and the eternal joy to be found there."[29]

Of course, some are deprived of this preview because they have not known a happy home since their forgotten premortal days. Many couples belong together who mistakenly think they must separate. Many families could be happy together every day, but they cannot imagine it, and their reflexes hardly permit an hour of harmony. For them there is no beautiful wrapping to caress, no encouraging shape to suggest the family possibilities of heaven. For that reason, the world needs all the happy homes it can get. The "privilege and the duty of every Latter-day Saint" is to provide, in this groping world, homes that are genuinely and visibly happy.

Among the faithful, clues can be moving. James E. Faust shared this panorama: "We see the vision of the heavenly hosts unnumbered whose eternal odysseys have been suspended as they wait for their vicarious work to be done, including the purification of baptism, the hollowed blessings of the endowment, and the exalting beatitude of sealings."

Then, when we have ordered their cause and prepared the way, these waiting ones of the spirit world will finally have their appointment to join us in the temple, where we have someone stand in for each family member. The picture is completed with this scene: "We can see families dancing, shouting, and crying with joy in being united in another world."[30] You and I, though we have solid clues, cannot quite imagine the happiness.

In addition to the "sociality," as a revelation calls it—referring to the warm personal connection we have with each other—we will have "eternal glory, which glory we do not now enjoy" (D&C 130:2). We don't have it now, so once again we have a clue that we don't quite grasp. But the prophets have elaborated. Lorenzo Snow explained that "we will have our bodies glorified, made free from every sickness and distress, and rendered most beautiful." And he added this interesting point: "There is nothing more beautiful to look upon than a resurrected man or woman."[31]

We do what we can to look nice, for we have a deep sense of what we were and will be. But mortal beauty is nothing more than a clue. Perfect form and features will be granted to every one in the day of resurrection. Heaven is, more than we can now comprehend, a place of beauty and joy.

90.
A MAGIC WORTH EVERYTHING

Crowns, thrones, exaltations,
and dominions are in reserve for
thee in the eternal worlds, and
the way is opened for thee to
return to the presence of thy
Heavenly Father. . . . The cup
is within thy reach; drink then
the heavenly draught and live.
—John Taylor[32]

A little eighteen-month-old boy fell into a large tub of water and, unable to push himself back out, drowned. The parents felt that their whole world ended by the sudden absence of that one little person they had known but a year and a half. Though they went on with life, the decades could not dim their magical longing, their nearly worshipful awe and devotion.

We can almost picture that son, whisked into the spirit realm and living there far more as man than boy, continuing to watch for his two devoted fans, his earthly parents whom he loves with a feeling much like worship. Do we suppose this sacred affection between couple and son could ever dim, no matter if the decades became centuries or gathered into thousands of years?

What magical attraction fills parents as they look upon their newborn babe? Beings who hardly know each other—strangers as far as this world is concerned, members of separate generations, who have only just met—take such unselfish posture, look with such a single eye, exert such laser-like attention toward each other. They do this with ease, as if drinking from a cup of joy.

The word *worship* is too strong. *Reverence* is not far from the mark—so intense, so open to love, so much more than mere courtesy or respect. We think too of the ready and unreserved yearning of the new child for its parents. And so, parent for child and child for parent, here is something more than admiration. Here is veneration, reverence, delight, awe—a cup of joy.

These same words describe the drawing power between husband and wife, groom and bride. As we try to measure the marvel of parent-child love, as we try to glimpse the miracle of family affection in general, we must not forget the magic that began those other ties: the divinely designed binding of man to woman.

The thirst for sacred joy draws us to each other—bride and groom, child and parent, generation to generation, heart to lineage, ancestor to descendant—a magical thirst God planted in his children to help them delight in each other. When family affection is at work, God's work may not be complete, but it has begun. And if they want to stay together forever? That is just what the Father hopes.

He hopes we will place our tender relationships at home far above worldly concerns. Gordon B. Hinckley said to couples, "Be fiercely loyal one to another."[33] That is no overstatement; it is the divine will. When the Lord commanded husband and wife to "cleave" to each other—adhere and never part, stick like glue, being welded and sealed one to another—he was giving us the eternal pattern, as couples are in celestial glory (Genesis 2:24; D&C 42:22).

To gain the whole world and lose the cup of joy would be the ultimate loss; to secure our families, the ultimate joy. The cup is within our reach.

91.
THE CYCLE OF SERVICE AND JOY

We lose our life by serving and lifting others. By so doing we experience the only true and lasting happiness. Service is not something we endure on this earth so we can earn the right to live in the celestial kingdom. Service is the very fiber of which an exalted life in the celestial kingdom is made. Oh, for the glorious day when these things all come naturally because of the purity of our hearts. . . . We are truly happy only when we are engaged in unselfish service. . . . Service is what godhood is all about.

—Marion G. Romney[34]

A frank young man named Stan once piped up in a Church class, "I'm not so sure I want to be exalted." Several other students looked up and seemed to hold their breath in surprise, wondering how the teacher would respond to such an unusual thought.

"Let me guess," the teacher smiled. "Too much responsibility. Too much work. Right?"

"Yeah, you got it," Stan answered. "In fact, way too much. I have a hard time just putting up with my busboy job in a little café! Why would I want to be cleaning up the whole universe?" With some relief, others in the class chuckled but then grew quiet as they realized that this really was a good point.

"I'm going to tell you two secrets, okay?" the teacher replied. "First, celestial people don't find it hard to do what they do. Remember, they have all power, and their minds are infinite. Nothing taxes their strength or their thoughts."

Stan asked, "You mean they don't run around sweating and forgetting

204

customers' names and nearly breaking everything because they're always in a hurry?"

The teacher's voice was soft and certain. "No, Stan. Think of our Father. Never in a hurry. Always at peace. He oversees everything and cares about everybody. It doesn't give him a headache." While the class thought about that, the teacher turned to 1 Nephi 1:14. "After seeing how things really are, Lehi said to God, 'Great and marvelous are thy works, O Lord God Almighty! Thy throne is high in the heavens, and thy power, and goodness, and mercy are over all the inhabitants of the earth.'"

The teacher looked at Stan and then at the other students. "See? That's the way our Father is, and that's the power he gives to exalted beings."

"Okay," Stan said, "what's the other secret?"

"Ah, the other secret," the teacher said as his eyes narrowed. "The first one, about exalted beings having all that ability is pretty obvious once you think about it, right?" Several in the class nodded. "But this next one, well, we've all heard it before, but for some reason it slips right out of our heads. We just kind of naturally forget all about it."

The teacher leaned forward and spoke in a near whisper. "So don't be shocked, okay?" More nods.

"God enjoys what he does," the teacher said with a bit of emotion. "Don't you all remember? 'When we're helping, we're happy.'[35] That's the big secret, and yet we've been singing it out loud since we were kids. Exalted beings have a fulness of joy because that's what they do all the time. They have all that power, and they use it to help others."

92.
WORTH ALL
WE POSSESS

Celestial glory is worth all we possess; if it calls for every dollar we own and our lives into the bargain, if we obtain an entrance into the celestial kingdom of God it will amply repay us. . . . If we can only manage to be faithful enough to obtain an inheritance in the kingdom, where God and Christ dwell, we shall rejoice through the endless ages of eternity.
—Wilford Woodruff[36]

The reason "celestial glory is worth all we possess" is not simply because of its location, furnishings, or powers but rather because of the beings who will be sharing it with us. Loved ones and friends we knew in mortal life? Yes. But a long and stunning list of others as well. Brigham Young pointed out that mortal life grooms us to "enjoy the society of Enoch, Noah, Melchizedek, Abraham, Isaac, and Jacob, or of their faithful children, and of the faithful Prophets and Apostles."

Of course, we have to be groomed as well as they were. Experience must prepare us as thoroughly as it prepared them. The life of each faithful person is carefully monitored to fill this purpose: "Every trial and experience you have passed through is necessary for your salvation."[37]

Brigham Young illustrated our quest with this comparison: "To give you a figure: I will say to a man, for instance, 'If you will go to Big Cottonwood [Canyon] blindfolded, I will give you a reward of ten thousand dollars. But you cannot have it if you go with your eyes open.' . . . The man starts blindfolded, fearing and trembling lest he shall run afoul of wild cattle, into ditches and difficulties. Yet he gropes his way and gets through, claims his reward and gets it. So [it is] in the dealings of the Lord with us. He does not let us see everything in the future before us, but makes us promises and makes us walk by faith that we may obtain them. And the greater our trials and conquests, the greater will be our crown and glory."[38]

We are not the only ones who ever stumbled and clambered along in life, having to rely on the friendship of God. History's greatest heroes did the same. That is how they sealed their friendship with him. They got acquainted with him in the dark, in emergencies, and in perils of every kind. To be ready to dwell with those heroes, we must have that sort of experience with him.

Thus, the mortal quest is not only to survive. It is not only to be happy. As the great Jehovah announced long ago, the mission of mortals would be to "do all things whatsoever the Lord their God shall command them" (Abraham 3:25). Joseph Smith called the earthly mission an "inquiry," a quest for "the knowledge of God." So a sign of success is not what we have but what we know—or whom we know—on emerging from this life.

Joseph then said of those who have succeeded in the past, "The inquiry frequently terminated, indeed always terminated when rightly pursued, in the most glorious discoveries."[39] No wonder, then, that Jesus said the essence of eternal life is "that they might know thee the only true God, and Jesus Christ" (John 17:3). It is our privilege to befriend the most elite Companions of all. That discovery is worth all we possess.

93.
WE SAW THE RISING VISTAS

We shouted for joy that an earth was to be prepared whereon we should dwell. Not one of us was whipped here; we came gladly and willingly, although undoubtedly we knew that it meant sorrow, distress, pain and ultimate death. We knew also that beyond this vale there would be a grand future, for we had seen the vistas of the future rising endlessly onward and upward, even to the very throne of God.

—Melvin J. Ballard [40]

Most mountains are shaped so that you cannot see the top if you are standing at the bottom. And those acquainted with mountain ranges know that when you are on one peak, higher peaks may still be hidden from view. Nestled beyond rising ridges and crests, the upper heights are visible either from a great way off or not until you reach them after ascending slope after slope and passing through canyon after canyon. The journey is worth it. For one thing, there are great adventures en route. And once you arrive, you see beauty beyond anything you have known. Only then is your view unhindered. Only when your climb is complete can you see so far.

From a distance, Mount Sinai is a magnificent, stately pillar of rock, towering over desert hills and deltas. But from its lower benches, the peak cannot be seen. Long hours did the eighty-year-old Moses hike its lesser peaks, carefully skirt countless massive boulders, traverse through or around gaping crevasses, and scale steep smooth slopes of stone. He knew the direction but did not glimpse the goal during all his ascent. Finally, as if appearing by surprise in the last hundred paces or so, there it was. He was on the summit, from which he could look out upon his two and a half million fellow Israelites camped in the desert valleys on every side. And there he saw and received far more, enough to save those millions and their future billions.

Each candidate for salvation must be a Moses. Each has the privilege of ascending lesser peaks and at long last taking those surprising one hundred paces or so into the presence of the God of Moses. Along the way will be one canyon after another to cross, one thrilling scene after another to stop and behold. There will be plenty to learn about on the ascent. There will be temptations to give up the climb. There will be time to think and countless occasions to stop and plead with heaven for strength to make the next ridge.

From the plains of Wyoming west of America's continental divide, the pioneers saw the sparkling heights of the Rocky Mountains. Most had seen mountains in their homelands. But this magnetic and majestic sight gave little hint of what lay ahead for them. Pitching their tents each night, they looked out at that layered range standing crisp against the orange sunset. Weeks passed, and they were in the foothills. They had lost sight of the mountaintops. Then came the arduous canyons full of trees and brush and the all-day climbs up steep grades of sage and loose shale. This mountain travel seemed endless until, almost suddenly, they reached the summit. With unspeakable joy, they saw their new home.

Long ago, we saw the goal. The splendid details could be known only by being there, but we could see the sparkling peaks. There awaited us then, and there await us yet, rising vistas. We will enjoy each one, and then, almost by surprise, we will be at the summit, "the very throne of God."

94.
THE GUARANTEE IS SURE

The gospel is also a power in itself. It is a creative power which gives man not alone dominion in the world, but the power, if he can attain it by his faith, to ordain and create other worlds. . . . Though man may not have in this life an occasion to exercise all the powers that come to him through the enrichment of his faith, those powers may be exercised in their fullness in eternity, if not in time.
—Joseph F. Smith[41]

The gospel is a dedicated and powerful system for saving— the Father's offer to transform his children from awkward and faltering into perfect and omnipotent. Though this seems an impossible aim, the plan works. How can we know that? By the power of the Holy Ghost.

We have another evidence that the plan works: "Our Father has passed through these ordeals, and has trodden the paths we are treading," declared Daniel H. Wells. "He kept his second estate, and has attained to his exaltation. We have the privilege of following in his footsteps."[42]

The plan we now follow has proven dependable for eons. The Father, a living being who interacts with us, is absolute evidence that the plan works. The world would be surprised at such an idea, but when we come to think of it, we find it reasonable and self-evident. God is living proof that his gospel has power to create exalted beings.

The world would also be surprised at how he shares his power with us, channeling it to earthly beings "in the ordinances thereof" (D&C 84:20).

Had he not clarified this, we might have been a long time guessing it. After all, the release of that power is quiet and usually flows in modest amounts.

The gospel changes a heart far more quickly than it perfects a whole life. But if we are observant, we notice over the years that increases of goodness and strength are marked by the times when, in the chapel, in the home, and in the temple, we once again receive the gospel ordinances. No wonder our leaders have occasionally made statements like this one from Marion G. Romney: "The power emanating from temples is far greater than we realize."[43]

The ordinances are magnificent despite their simplicity. They are bestowed often, which is no reason to take them lightly but is precisely why they are so potent. Our Father has made them necessary to exalted life. Moral perfection is mandatory, of course, but even that could not be had without the ordinances.

Joseph Smith assured us that "the law of heaven . . . guarantees to all who obey it a reward far beyond any earthly consideration."[44] If we will be patient with the price—the laws and ordinances—the reward is guaranteed.

Unlike some man-made guarantees, this one will not disappoint the customer. In fact, the gospel guarantee is an understatement, for we will receive—and become—much more than we could ask or expect or imagine. As Joseph F. Smith said, even the most righteous person "may not have in this life an occasion to exercise all the powers that come to him through the enrichment of his faith."

We receive more, not less, than we are promised. There is no way to try out the wings of exaltation during our mortal test. But in a day more real than the present, "those powers may be exercised in their fullness." Such is the gospel guarantee.

95.
WE HAVE
TIME

You must begin with the first, and go on until you learn all the principles of exaltation. But it will be a great while after you have passed through the veil before you will have learned them. It is not all to be comprehended in this world; it will be a great work to learn our salvation and exaltation even beyond the grave.

—Joseph Smith[45]

Now and then we hear Church members muse on whether there is such a thing as "time" in eternity. Whatever sort of time we will have in eternity, we can do little about the matter now. Our present life is all about time. Everything we have been asked to do takes time. It is good to know that we have time to do it all.

One of Brigham Young's daughters, Susa, wrote this of her father: "Brigham Young went always on his calm, deliberate way, exceedingly kind and gentle to his family, thoughtful of his friends, indifferent to his enemies, and above all never hurried nor worried. It is significant that just after the martyrdom [of Joseph Smith], President Young dreamed he saw Brother Joseph who told him not to be in a hurry—this admonition was given thrice. In all his years he never forgot that advice. 'If this people want wealth, comfort, and happiness, do not be in a hurry,' he said."[46]

Brigham gave that advice often and lived it so well that he hardly had to say it at all. "'Do not hurry me,' is one of the prominent characteristics of my history," he once said. "I frequently exhort the brethren *not to be in a hurry,* for we shall not stop here, we are only hunting for the grave."[47]

On another occasion, he pointed out that "when we have lived, and gathered around us more kingdoms and creations than it is possible for the mind of mortals to comprehend, . . . when you have reached this stage in the onward course of your progression, you will be perfectly satisfied not to be in a hurry."[48]

God is not hasty. He is never frantic. He would prefer that we not be frantic either. Haste comes of fear, the opposite of faith.

We note in Joseph Smith's statement that "the principles of exaltation" are learned slowly. Evidently there is a lot to them, more than we can imagine. So we will have to master them "a great while after [passing] through the veil." Only on the other side of that barrier—when our abilities are equal to the great shoreline of truth and only when we have teachers who are distinctly advanced, messengers from the other side of the great expanse—can we hope to learn those principles.

The things we will someday know as a matter of course are "not all to be comprehended in this world" because mortal brains are just not keen enough. But that's all right. We are here for another work, getting quality into our souls. We have time for that. And when we have taken care of quality, we will have plenty of time for the quantity and the comprehending.

When it comes time for learning advanced principles, it will, as Joseph Smith taught, be "a great work," reserved for a time "beyond the grave." But first things first. For now, we have important things to occupy our precious time.

96.
THE RIGHT SEED

The witness of the Spirit to you, my brethren and sisters, is that you are the offspring of the Lord, that the spirits which inhabit your bodies are immortal, and that in due time, if you are faithful, you will go back to the presence of that God who gave you life.

—George Albert Smith[49]

A seed doesn't have to contain everything a tree contains. It will add new materials as it needs them. What a seed needs is the right blueprint or recipe for the tree it is going to be. The miracle of a seed is that as moisture soaks into its skin and as it draws upon sunlight, it builds root and stem and all else, passing patiently through each stage of growth.

There is a tree whose seed is so small that two hundred of them hide in a cone the size of an egg, so light that 100,000 of them weigh only a pound. Yet one of these seeds can yield, from the light and elements around it, an enormous phenomenon of nature, a giant sequoia—*Sequoiadendron Giganteum*, the largest of all trees. The mature tree may live two thousand years or more, grow taller than a twenty-six-story skyscraper, become so wide that it could block three lanes of traffic, and weigh more than three blue whales. One tiny flake-like seed—delicate, lighter than cotton, almost too small to pick up without tweezers—grows to two billion times its size and hundreds of billions of times its weight. If we could look closely, we might see a bright "S" written on it, standing for "Supertree."

More remarkable than the Supertree miracle is the miracle of man, seed of the Man of Holiness (Moses 6:57). Someone so frail, so uninformed, and so undeveloped as the infant child of God is able to draw into himself just the right materials, in just the right sequence, for becoming a being quite unlike the early version. This seed of God needs time, patient care, and lots of light and living water for the greatest marvel in the universe to unfold. Each human infant is a Supersoul. Tiny miracle by miracle, Man—*Soul Giganteum,* we might call our race—gradually, naturally becomes as the infinite and holy Father who planted all this potential in us to begin with.

This is true of every human soul. Not one revelation implies that some of the Father's children cannot become as he is. Once we have seen any of them dramatically change at their core—even unlikely ones like the crafty Zeezrom, the rebellious Alma, or the raging Saul—we know it is entirely possible for anyone to change. When Alma and Saul left this world, they were pointed in the right direction. Their hearts were right. The living waters had soaked in, the light was acting upon them, the right elements were being gathered. They were not yet towering sequoias in eternity, not yet billions of times their original size. But they are still growing. They have plenty of time.

The crowberry, the world's smallest pine tree, is also beautiful. But forest gods called sequoias do not grow from crowberry seeds. To get a forest god or a real god, you must start out with the right seed. You *are* starting out with the right seed. Each soul of mankind may become *Soul Giganteum.* We don't have to start out any more superhuman than we already are.

215

97.
LONG STAIRWAY, SMALL STEPS

Remember, you can be exalted without a college degree. You can be exalted without being slender and beautiful. You can be exalted without having a successful career. You can be exalted if you are not rich and famous. So focus the best that you can on those things in life that will lead you back to the presence of God—keeping all things in their proper balance.
—M. Russell Ballard [50]

Ten-year-old Jeannie looked up at the great pyramid temple, one of several among the ruins of Tikal. Its apex stood higher than the awesome trees of the surrounding jungle. "This is the one we climb," her dad announced.

"But it's too high for me," Jeannie answered quietly. Her father might have brushed off that comment, but he noticed that Jeannie's lower lip was trembling and that moisture was brimming from her eyes.

"Do you see that rock over there?" he asked. Jeannie turned and saw the stone, about ten inches high, in some nearby rubble. Her father walked over and stood by it. "Come stand on it, will you?" She hopped up on the stone and looked up at her father. He stooped down, put his hands on his knees and looked into her eyes with a smile. "Jeannie, all the steps on that pyramid are about the same size as this stone." She looked up at the stairs that led to the apex and back down at the stone where she was standing. "Do you think you can step up on each of them, one at a time, just like you did this rock here?" he asked. Jeannie looked way up at the apex again and smiled.

Riley, soon to turn fourteen, was meeting with his bishop. "I'm glad you're living a worthy life, Riley. So, are you willing to fill the duties of a teacher in the Aaronic Priesthood?"

A bit timidly, Riley asked, "Like what?"

"Well," the bishop smiled, "someone has to come early before sacrament meeting and set up the sacrament table, get the bread ready, and fill the cups with water. The Lord says that should be the teachers." Riley looked at the floor, remembering how hard it was just to get to the meetings at all. The bishop went on, "And then there's that word *teacher*. As a teacher, you'll be assigned with a Melchizedek Priesthood holder to visit some families each month."

Riley's head came up. "You mean be a home teacher?" The bishop nodded. "I have to say something? I'm supposed to teach?"

It hadn't been easy to accept those responsibilities, but Riley decided he would. A few days later, at the time of his ordination, he was given a blessing of strength. He would be equal to this new office. "You will receive added callings as the years go by, Riley," he was told. "Someday you will have responsibilities you can't imagine right now. But let your mind be at peace about the future. No step will ever be more difficult than the one you are taking today. You will always be able to take the next step."

There are a lot of steps, but they are taken one at a time. They are small enough for anyone. We don't have to be amazing. We don't have to be impressive to the world or even known to the world in order to impress our Father and receive his all. We just have to keep taking steps.

98.
CHOOSE THE RIGHT PRIZE

*When earth life is over and
things appear in their true perspective, we shall more clearly see
. . . that the fruits of the gospel
are the only objectives worthy of
life's full efforts. . . . I conceive the
blessings of the gospel to be of
such inestimable worth that the
price for them must be very exacting. . . . The price, however, is
within the reach of us all, because
it is not to be paid in money nor
in any of this world's goods but in
righteous living. What is required
is wholehearted devotion to the
gospel and unreserved allegiance
to the Church of Jesus Christ of
Latter-day Saints.*

—Marion G. Romney[51]

From the top of the pyramid,
Jeannie and her father gazed
over the lush jungle. It was a
clear day, and it seemed to Jeannie
that they could see all of the world, or
at least all of Guatemala. Parrots
fluttered now and then above the
leafy canopy below them, their gor-
geous feathers flashing in the sun.
Occasionally a tuft of branches would
dip out of place, and with her father's
binoculars Jeannie could just detect
the dark movements of a howler mon-
key or a family of timid spider mon-
keys. After they had taken pictures
and had been in the heat long enough,
her father asked, "How about if we go
down now? There is still a lot more to
see, you know."

But Jeannie didn't want to leave.
"I had no idea it would be like this,"
she said with wonder.

"Just an hour ago," her father
chuckled, "you didn't even want to
come up here."

"I know," she answered. She was
now watching an eagle circle over-
head. And she said it again. "But I
had no idea it would be so wonderful."

Those words have been spoken by

millions. They have been muttered by people who were once afraid to ride a bicycle or ride in a plane. There is little point in trying to tell someone what it is like to swim along the bottom of a clear lake if that person is afraid of the water. He will just have to go there and find out for himself. It is hard to explain the mission of parenthood to one who is frightened of having a baby. She will not know the joy until she has her own child.

Riley, who once hesitated to become a teacher in the Aaronic Priesthood, said to himself, "I had no idea it would be like this" when he performed his first baptism in the mission field and when he signed on later to be a seminary teacher.

We mortals are not good at picturing in the mind any reality we have not known before. And yet, the best realities are especially so—outside our experience, impossible to imagine. If the prize is cheap or if we can imagine it beforehand, it probably is not worth the price.

The gospel prize is, as Marion G. Romney said, "very exacting." That is, it calls for "life's full efforts." Strangely, we are free to pay that price for a paltry prize if we choose, and some do just that. We will have to give all of our years, all of our waking time and money and strength to some prize or another. Life's full efforts are easy enough to give. They must be given, even if to nothing more than an overstuffed chair or a shelf full of videos. The key is not paying the price but choosing the right prize. Those who choose well, who choose to give their all for the gospel prize, will be the ones saying, "I had no idea it would be so wonderful."

99.
THE PLEASING WORK OF MERCY

The time will come when many people whom we now regard perhaps as not entitled to great consideration will be blessed beyond our capacity to understand. Hasn't [God] told us that the very least of the blessings which come to men in his kingdom will so far surpass our conception of blessing and mercy that the minds of men cannot conceive of it?

—Anthony W. Ivins[52]

The promise of mercy, which will be expressed so bountifully in the gift of exaltation, is the key to all promises, the master promise. Mercy is the theme, the heartthrob of the people of promise.

We once had a visitor in our home who could hardly stop expressing her troubled and critical feelings. At one point she said with passion, "And here's another thing. I cannot stand people with racial prejudice. Who do they think they are, looking down on others? I can't stand to be around them. I hate them!" Very quietly, and with a little smile, my wife inquired, "Let me see if I understand. Are you saying that you hate people who hate people?"

Amazingly, we tend to draw the line with our mercy. We tend to make the circle of grace pretty small. For example, we may choose to love everybody except for those who don't love everybody. But, as Brigham Young reminded us:

"The Lord is more merciful to the people than we are, . . . while we . . . have a disposition . . . that is revengeful, and apt to give way to passion, wrath, malice, anger, bickering, contentions, hateful feelings and unbecoming words. All men are subject to this; but the Latter-day Saints should be above it; and I wish to caution them, and to inform them that if they expect to enter the celestial kingdom they must overcome this weakness."[53]

We can't afford to be like the children on the playground who "catch" each other breaking the rules. It isn't right to break rules, but one of our rules, one of the standards for adulthood in spiritual matters, is that we not find fault, that we overcome our tendency to catch each other being bad (D&C 88:124). We can't even afford to catch each other catching each other.

Our imperfect eyes view mankind with opinions very different from our Father's. "Our heavenly Father," Joseph Smith taught, "is more liberal in His views, and boundless in His mercies and blessings, than we are ready to believe or receive."[54] In fact, we are mistaken if we look with despair at that person we see in the mirror. Eyes that look outwardly with poor vision at others, in the light of day, may not discern the inward self very well either. In truth, there is enormous grace for those who struggle.

The merciful, the experts on mercy, are the ones who receive the greatest gift of mercy, the inestimable gift of exaltation (Matthew 5:7). That is as it should be, for these are the ones who will operate as God does, with infinite kindness and patience, throughout the ages to come.

"God is more merciful than man is, he possesses more sympathies with human nature than man does or ever did, one with another,"[55] said John Taylor. While God's children find fault with each other, God is zealously, kindly working to get them ready for eternity. That will be our pleasing work and glory forever if we will make it our work and glory now.

100.
CHILDREN OF LIGHT

God has created man with a mind capable of instruction, and a faculty which may be enlarged in proportion to the heed and diligence given to the light communicated from heaven to the intellect; and . . . the nearer man approaches perfection, the clearer are his views, and the greater his enjoyments, till he has overcome the evils of his life and lost every desire for sin; and like the ancients, arrives at that point of faith where he is wrapped in the power and glory of his Maker and is caught up to dwell with Him.

—Joseph Smith[56]

The Lord sometimes refers to his people as "children of light" (Luke 16:8; John 12:36; 1 Thessalonians 5:5; D&C 106:5). This title is a kind of invitation, an offer. If we turn away from darkness, and hunger for light, he will make sure we receive it.

Light will enlarge and transform us. Thanks to light, the sequoia seed transforms to four hundred billion times its starting weight. If weight could be compared to time and the seed were a second, the mature tree would be twelve thousand years old. Nature teaches us a lesson about those delicate and well-mannered rays of light.

The light that supports nature radiates generously from the sun. But it does not insist. It can so easily be blocked. It has to be received, invited, sought. The tree must stretch upward, climb and reach, train its many surfaces toward the sun.

The other light, the finer kind that supports and enlarges our souls, flows liberally from the Son of God (Matthew 5:45; James 1:5; D&C 88:12). Yet, with little effort we can put up barriers and live in shadows

(Moses 5:21–22). If we want light, we reach up and receive it. Then we will grow dramatically and automatically because of who we are—because of who our Father is.

If we are light friendly, it stays in us and builds us. In the resurrection, we then harvest all of those years of reaching upward: "They who are of a celestial spirit shall receive the same body which was a natural body; even ye shall receive your bodies, and your glory shall be that glory by which your bodies are quickened. Ye who are quickened by a portion of the celestial glory shall then receive of the same, even a fulness" (D&C 88:28–29).

Consider the Nephites living at the time of Christ's death. The signs were so severe that only the more righteous survived, and these were literally shaken into a new phase of life. They emerged from their long night hungry for light. It bade them refine their lives as it bids all of us. In the months that followed they repented thoroughly, rebuilding their culture from the inside out. They were "enlarged in proportion to the heed and diligence given to the light communicated from heaven to the intellect." Responding to light, they grew like sequoias until they could endure the glorious presence of Jesus. So he came among them (3 Nephi 9:13; 10:18; 19:25). At his feet, they were filled even further, "wrapped in the power and glory of [their] Maker."

That quiet, wonderful pattern is always available. But we must get out of the shadows. We must hunger, thirst, have our eyes single, plead, and invite in order to be filled with the light of the Spirit (3 Nephi 12:6; D&C 88:67–68). It drives out sorrow and sin, preparing us for "the Father of lights" (James 1:17; D&C 67:9). It fashions us to be as he is. All the promises will be kept. The children of the promise "bear his presence in the world of glory" (D&C 76:118). We will become children of light.

101.
CONCLUSION: THE PROMISES ARE SURE

He has the power to keep His promises. It is my testimony to you that He does so.
—Gordon B. Hinckley[57]

The bishop was soon to be released. I asked him, "What's the biggest thing you've learned?" He answered easily, "My mother asked me that a few years ago. I told her I'd learned that this is the Lord's church, not the bishop's. I still see that all the time. But there is something else. I realize more than ever that God is a covenant person. I don't know where I got that term, but it keeps coming to mind. He keeps his promises, and he wants us to keep ours."

He continued, "People who make the covenants and don't keep them, they get into bad territory. It seems like their homes are under Satan's thumb. Those who keep their covenants have problems too, but somehow they can move on and be happy and have peace. God seems to be with them even when life is hard. That's why I call him a covenant person."

A bishop, working with real people, could see God's hand. In the work of that hand he could see God's nature. "[God] will never desert us," said George Q. Cannon. "He cannot do it."[58] Because he is perfectly trustworthy, his promises get our attention.

They tell us about real possibilities within our reach. When God speaks a promise, our hearts awaken and our minds take note.

In the *Lectures on Faith* presented to early Church leaders, Joseph Smith reasoned carefully, "And lastly, but not less important to the exercise of faith in God, is the idea of the existence of the attribute truth in him." Joseph emphasized what a difference it makes if we really trust the honesty of God. "No sooner is the idea of the existence of this attribute planted in the minds of men, than it gives power to the mind. . . . They are enabled by faith to lay hold on the promises which are set before them, and wade through all the tribulations and afflictions."[59]

Joseph spoke from experience. His own endurance could be traced to his faith in the honesty of God. Those who heard him teach that principle later faced their own "tribulations and afflictions." We must learn by experience to trust God. Armed with that confidence, we merit further promises.

The monthly "test"-imony meeting is a part of this cycle, when "test" results come in. The faithful report after testing the promises of God. Their lab reports are conclusive. It turns out that gospel living is more than a class or a meeting. It is our experience with God's faithfulness and his experience with our faithfulness. He makes promises, we make promises. We keep ours, he keeps his. Mighty faith emerges in us. We have confidence in him, and he has confidence in us.

Marion G. Romney pleaded with the young in faith: "Believe in and live for the promises of the Lord by keeping his commandments. If you will do this," he promised, "even though you do not now have full confidence in those promises, I assure you that that confidence will come."[60] As we grow older in the faith, our conclusion is that the promises are sure.

Notes

1. Brigham Young, in *Journal of Discourses,* 26 vols. (London: Latter-day Saints' Book Depot, 1854–86), 1:353.
2. James E. Talmage, in *Collected Discourses,* comp. Brian H. Stuy, 5 vols. (Burbank, Calif.: B.H.S. Publishing, 1987–92), 3:291.
3. Ibid.
4. Joseph F. Smith, in *Messages of the First Presidency,* ed. James R. Clark, 6 vols. (Salt Lake City: Bookcraft, 1965–75), 5:6–7.
5. L. Tom Perry, "Becoming Men in Whom the Spirit of God Is," *Ensign,* May 2002, 41.
6. George Q. Cannon, in *Collected Discourses,* 2:143–44.
7. Wilford Woodruff, *Wilford Woodruff's Journal,* ed. Scott G. Kenney, 9 vols. (Midvale, Utah: Signature Books, 1983), 3:252–53.
8. John Taylor, in *Messages of the First Presidency,* 2:299.
9. This quote and those that follow are from Brigham Young's sermon at the funeral of Jedediah M. Grant, in *Journal of Discourses,* 4:131–34.
10. Brigham Young, in *Journal of Discourses,* 6:347.
11. John Taylor, *Mediation and Atonement* (Salt Lake City: Deseret News Company, 1882), 158.
12. Joseph Fielding Smith, *Doctrines of Salvation,* comp. Bruce R. McConkie, 3 vols. (Salt Lake City: Bookcraft, 1954–56), 3:59.
13. Lorenzo Snow, in *Collected Discourses,* 3:363.
14. Wilford Woodruff, in *Journal of Discourses,* 16:269.
15. Melvin J. Ballard, in Bryant S. Hinckley, *Sermons and Missionary Services of Melvin J. Ballard* (Salt Lake City: Deseret Book, 1949), 233.
16. Rudger Clawson, in Conference Reports of The Church of Jesus Christ of Latter-day Saints (Salt Lake City: The Church of Jesus Christ of Latter-day Saints, 1898 to present), October 1908, 74.
17. Heber J. Grant, in Conference Report, October 1919, 23.
18. Brigham Young, in *Journal of Discourses,* 8:208.
19. Joseph Smith, *Teachings of the Prophet Joseph Smith,* sel. Joseph Fielding Smith (Salt Lake City: Deseret Book, 1976), 301.
20. James E. Talmage, "The Eternity of Sex," *Young Woman's Journal,* October 1914, 604.
21. James E. Talmage, "Our Lord the Christ," *Improvement Era,* December 1932, 69.
22. "We Thank Thee, O God, for a Prophet," *Hymns of The Church of Jesus Christ of Latter-day Saints* (Salt Lake City: The Church of Jesus Christ of Latter-day Saints, 1985), no. 19.
23. Bruce R. McConkie, in Joseph Fielding McConkie and Robert L. Millet, *Joseph Smith: The Choice Seer* (Salt Lake City: Bookcraft, 1996), 337–38.
24. Brigham Young, in *Journal of Discourses,* 17:142.

25. Joseph B. Wirthlin, "Follow Me," *Ensign*, May 2002, 17.

26. Melvin J. Ballard, in *Sermons and Missionary Services of Melvin Joseph Ballard*, 156.

27. Joseph Smith, *Lectures on Faith* (Salt Lake City: Deseret Book, 1985), 4:45.

28. Lorenzo Snow, in Conference Report, October 1900, 4.

29. Thomas S. Monson, "Bring Him Home," *Ensign*, November 2003, 57.

30. James E. Faust, "Who Shall Ascend into the Hill of the Lord," *Ensign*, August 2001, 4.

31. Lorenzo Snow, in Conference Report, October 1900, 4.

32. John Taylor, *Gospel Kingdom*, sel. G. Homer Durham, 1st ed. (Salt Lake City: Bookcraft, 1943), 14.

33. Gordon B. Hinckley, "Messages of Inspiration from President Hinckley," *Church News*, 2 September 1995, 2.

34. Marion G. Romney, "The Celestial Nature of Self-Reliance," *Ensign*, June 1984, 6.

35. "When We're Helping," *Children's Songbook* (Salt Lake City: The Church of Jesus Christ of Latter-day Saints, 1989), 198.

36. Wilford Woodruff, in *Journal of Discourses*, 17:250.

37. Brigham Young, in *Journal of Discourses*, 8:150–51.

38. Brigham Young, in *Wilford Woodruff's Journal*, 5:546–47.

39. Joseph Smith, *Lectures on Faith*, 2:56.

40. Melvin J. Ballard, "Redeemer," *Liahona, The Elders' Journal* 28 (23 December 1930): 320.

41. Joseph F. Smith, *Gospel Doctrine* (Salt Lake City: Deseret Book, 1975), 212–13.

42. Daniel H. Wells, in *Journal of Discourses*, 16:127.

43. Marion G. Romney, *Look to God and Live*, comp. George J. Romney (Salt Lake City: Deseret Book, 1975), 236.

44. Joseph Smith, *History of the Church*, 2:7.

45. Joseph Smith, *Teachings of the Prophet Joseph Smith*, 348.

46. Susa Young Gates, *The Life Story of Brigham Young* (New York: The Macmillan Company, 1931), 316.

47. Brigham Young, in *Journal of Discourses*, 1:92; emphasis in the original.

48. Ibid., 1:353.

49. George Albert Smith, in Conference Report, April 1905, 61.

50. M. Russell Ballard, "Be Strong in the Lord, and in the Power of His Might," *Brigham Young University 2001–2002 Speeches* (Provo, Utah: BYU Publications & Graphics, 2002), 228.

51. Marion G. Romney, in Conference Report, October 1949, 39, 43.

52. Anthony W. Ivins, "Is Persecution a Result of Transgression or Righteousness?" *Improvement Era*, March 1924, 413.

53. Brigham Young, in *Journal of Discourses*, 14:149.

54. Joseph Smith, *Teachings of the Prophet Joseph Smith*, 257.

55. John Taylor, in *Journal of Discourses*, 19:155.

56. Joseph Smith, *Teachings of the Prophet Joseph Smith*, 51.

57. Gordon B. Hinckley, " Messages of Inspiration from President Hinckley," *Church News*, 3 January 1998, 2.

58. George Q. Cannon, in *Collected Discourses,* 2:185.
59. Joseph Smith, *Lectures on Faith,* 4:16, 14.
60. Marion G. Romney, in Conference Report, October 1952, 35.

INDEX

A

Action, call to, 178–79
Adoption, 84–85
Agents, of children, 92–93
America, mission of, 124–25
Angels, 174–75
Antipus, 138–39
Art: raising children as, 86–87; kindness as, 109
Ashton, Marvin J., on having patience with family members, 91

B

Balance, 12–13
Ballard, M. Russell: on proclamations, 62; on choices in media, 106–7; on focusing on exaltation, 216
Ballard, Melvin J.: on tithing, 43; on Saints and world events, 117; on doing work for dead, 186; on being in Christ's presence, 199; on choice to come to earth, 208
Battle, for souls, 136–37
"Battle Hymn of the Republic, The," 124
Beauty, of future life, 200–201
Bedtime, setting, 20–21
Bennion, Adam S., on science and religion, 127
Bennion, Samuel O., on fast offerings, 45
Benson, Ezra Taft: on Book of Mormon, 24–25; on revelation in temple, 47; on trials, 48–49; on fears of provider, 78; on marriage, 82, 107; on scripture study, 99, 100, 151; on homes as heaven on earth, 105; on future of youth, 139
Blessings: keeping Sabbath and, 40–41; Heber J. Grant on, 42; of scripture study, 99; of nations, 122–23; keeping commandments and, 164–65
Book of Mormon: Ezra Taft Benson on, 24–25: family study of, 100–101; Bruce R McConkie on, 127; translation of, 154
Brown, Hugh B., on kingdom rolling forward, 132
Business, Sabbath day and, 40–41

C

Callings: being magnified by, 144–45; Dallin H. Oaks on, 151
Callis, Charles A., on living water, 54
Cannon, George Q.: on unity, 76; on timing and readiness, 155; on Lord's love, 176; on Lord's promises, 224
Caring, teaching and, 184–85
Catching up, marriage and children and, 82–83
Celestial glory: children in, 190–91; worth of, 206–7
Change, 162–63
Character: Spencer W. Kimall on thoughts and, 36; built by callings, 144–45; David O. McKay on escaping, 146
Charity, 52
Chastity, 68–69; as foundation of happy life, 32–33; as shield of virtue, 34–35; David O. McKay on, 71

231

D

E

F

importance of teaching, 153; on resurrected beings, 183

Smoot, Reed: on welcoming children, 84; on providing for children, 85

Snow, Lorenzo: on blessings through trials, 50; on preaching in spirit prison, 184; on hopes for future life, 200; on resurrected bodies, 201

Souls, building, 136–37

Spirit prison, teaching in, 184–85

Sports, 158–59

Stability, purpose and, 16–17

Stapely, Delbert L., on answers to prayers, 9

Stature, marriage and, 72–73

Status, marriage and, 73

Steps, taking small, 216–17

Sting, removing death of, 186–87

Stories: Johnsongrass, 37; comet, 66–67; man who turns down golf game, 75; couple with motor home, 136; Elder Casey Carter, 140–41; woman called to be Young Women president, 142–43; cutting firewood, 160–61; boy hanging from window, 192–93; busboy, 204–5; young man called as teacher, 217

Straight and narrow path, 194–95

Strength, in self and Church, 164–65

Suffering, joy and, 48–49

T

Talmage, James E.: on angels, 174; on deafness to spiritual things, 175; on eternal increase, 191; on knowledge of Christ, 192

Tanner, Nathan Eldon, on honoring self, 70

Taylor, John: on living religion, 5; on death of Brigham Young, 180; on priesthood beyond veil, 183; on eternal worlds, 202; on God's mercy, 221

Taylor, John W., on building kingdom of God, 55

Teaching, 152–53; in spirit prison, 184–85

Temple: ordinances of, 46–47; learning in, 47; home and, 102–3; man in, 188–89; Marion G. Romney on, 211

Temple work: for dead, 182–83, 186–87, 201; family and, 188–89

Temptation, resisting, 26–27, 28–29

Testimony: gaining, 8–9; Book of Mormon and, 24–25, 28–29

Thoughts: Spencer W. Kimball on, 22, 36; controlling, 28; resisting temptation through, 28–29; destiny and, 36–37; of servant, 150–51

Time: for meditation, 20–21; as offering, 137; in eternity, 212–13

Tithing, 42–43

Translation, of Book of Mormon, 154

Tree: weakened by supports, 78–79; seeds and, 214–15

Trials, 48–49, 196–97; drawing nearer to God through, 50–51; Lord's work and, 166–67

Triumph, of Church, 130–31

U

Uniqueness, of children, 92–93

Unity: marriage and, 76–77; power of, 154–55

Urgency, 161, 212–13

V

Virtue, chastity as shield of, 34–35

Voice of God, 2–3

W

Weeds, 37

Wells, Daniel H., on path of Heavenly Father, 210

Whitmer, David, on translation of Book of Mormon, 154

Whitney, Orson F., on mission of Church, 158

Widtsoe, John A.: on searching for truth, 8; on getting nearer to Lord, 18; on temple and home, 102–3

Wife, as provider, 78–79

Winning, Church and, 158–59

Wirthlin, Joseph B.: on house of faith, 160; on following Christ, 198

Women: honor of, 80–81; promised marriage and children, 82–83, 190–91

Woodruff, Wilford: on Holy Ghost, 10; on worth of eternal family, 66; on choice spirits in last days, 138; on call to action, 178; on spirit prison, 185; on celestial glory, 206

Word of God, 18–19, 99

Work, 140–41; in last days, 160–61; Lord's, 166–67; after death, 180–81

World events, Saints and, 117

Worth: of eternal family, 66–67; of celestial glory, 206–7

Y

Young, Brigham: on prison as palace, 19; on temptation, 26, 28, 29; on marriage, 72; on blessing of children, 83, 190; on obedient children, 89; on plan of salvation, 123; on worrying, 145; on eternity, 173; John Taylor on death of, 180; on work after death, 180–81; on doing work for dead, 182; on death, 196; on quest for celestial glory, 206–7; on hurrying, 212–13; on mercy, 220–21

Young, Brigham Jr., on family prayer, 94

Young, John, on leadership, 148

Young, Susa, on Brigham Young, 212

Youth, protection of, 162–63

Z

Zion, building up, 118–19

Zoo, author turns down job at, 39